George Seferis

Book of Exercises II

translated from Greek by Jennifer R. Kellogg

WORLD POETRY

Originally published in Greek as *Τετράδιο Γυμνασμάτων, Β'*
(Athens: Ikaros, 1976)

First Edition, First Printing, 2024
ISBN 978-1-954218-28-4

World Poetry Books
New York, NY
www.worldpoetrybooks.com

Available to the trade through Asterism Books
Distributed in the UK and Europe by Turnaround Publisher Services
Subscriptions and standing orders available directly from the publisher

Library of Congress Control Number: 2024943197

Cover Image: Yannis Moralis, detail from *"Painted Comments," illustration to the "Poems" of George Seferis published by Ikaros, 1965.* Oil pastel on paper. National Gallery, Alexandros Soutsos Museum.

Cover design by Andrew Bourne
Typesetting by Don't Look Now
Printed in Lithuania by BALTO Print

A publisher of exceptional translations of poetry from a broad range of languages and traditions, bringing the work of modern masters, emerging voices, and pioneering innovators from around the world to English-language readers in affordable trade editions, World Poetry Books is a 501(c)(3) nonprofit and charitable organization founded in 2017 in New York City, affiliated with the Humanities Institute and the Translation Program at the University of Connecticut (Storrs), and a member of the Community of Literary Magazines and Presses (CLMP).

Table of Contents

Circumstantial Poems (1931–1971)

***Calligraphies** (1941–1942)*

Translator's Introduction

> *I wandered, got tired, and wrote very little.*
>
> *But returning home was always on my mind—40 years.*
>
> *Man is an infant at all ages—*
>
> *in the cradle's tenderness and brutality.*
>
> *Like the shoreline and the sea, everything else is erased—*
>
> *our embrace and the sound of our voice.*

THE PROBLEM OF HOME dominated the professional and personal life of the journeying poet-diplomat George Seferis. Seferis wrote as both a representative of a government frequently in crisis and an artist seeking to assimilate his voice into the Greek poetic and oral tradition. Possibly written in 1954, the bittersweet poem above alludes to the fortieth anniversary of his family's flight from his birthplace in Smyrna (Izmir), Turkey, in 1914, at the outbreak of World War I. Like the 1.5 million refugees who would soon come to Greece during the war's aftermath, Seferis had to begin a new life under precarious conditions. He was protected by his father's connections to Greece's political leadership and the expectation that he would become a diplomat serving the Greek government.

Seferis began writing poetry under pseudonyms as a teenager. While studying in France, he wrote his first adolescent romantic verses under the name George Skaliotis. This alias referred to his maternal ancestors' village along the Aegean coast of Turkey, Skala tou Vourla (Urla). Skala's world of orchards, fishermen, and rural communality became a lifelong touchstone, conveying authenticity, tradition, and simplicity. "The faces of boats inhabit my life," he wrote in the poem "Argo," included in this volume. When his first book of poetry, *Turning*

Point, appeared in 1931, it was accompanied by the image of a mermaid with a forked tail, the boatman's good luck charm.

Seferis wrote often about his deliberately bifurcated self. One year into his career as a diplomat at age 27, he lamented that he would always have "two masters"—his government service and his calling as a poet. "The only inclination I have is that I want to make poems, patiently, stubbornly, working for months and years ... My external servitude will be a lifelong wound; it will keep me walled in." Yet this compartmentalization facilitated the successful discharge of what he perceived to be the duties of each role: unflagging, impersonal devotion to his country and mastery of the craft of poetry. In government work, he was George Seferiades, his birth name; in print, he was George Seferis, a pen name derived from *sefer*, the Turkish word for campaign or journey, meaning "wayfarer." It was Seferis who won the Nobel Prize in Literature in 1963 and Seferiades who served the Greek government through the totalitarian Metaxas regime, World War II, the Civil War, and the Cyprus crisis of the '50s and '60s.

Seferis is identified with the Generation of the '30s, a cohort of modernists who explored Greek identity through vernacular Greek language and culture while also assimilating Western European ideals and artistic forms. As a French- and English-speaking diplomat and poet, he exemplified this trend. His early work attempted to combine English modernist free verse and French symbolism with vernacular Greek, as opposed to the purified Greek, *katharevousa*, that was the official language of the Greek state. (The poems "Mr. Fatty A. Lovemaker," and "Ode in Bastardized Verse à la Kalvos" satirize *katharevousa*.) For Seferis, the authentic Greek language was spoken Greek as it evolved naturally through the diaspora. In his later work, Seferis sought to recapture a dying Greek folk culture through an encounter with Cyprus and spiritual revelation.

In early 1940, acutely aware that war would be arriving on Greece's doorstep at any moment, Seferis decided to self-publish three separate poetry books. "They will be the last that

I publish, as long as these conditions hold," he wrote in his journal. First, he created a single volume that included all of his work published through 1936; then, a second collection of unpublished poems written between 1928 and 1937 in London, Greece, and Albania, entitled *Book of Exercises*. Finally, he issued a third collection of new work written between 1937 and 1940 entitled *Logbook*, a reference to a ship captain's log. Two more *Logbooks* followed in 1944 and 1955, the first with poems from his time in Egypt and South Africa and the second from Cyprus. Seferis's poetry volumes took shape in transitional moments between journeys—"I wandered, got tired, and wrote very little," as the poem quoted above remarks. In his peripatetic life, he often noted the date and place of composition of each poem. For Seferis, poetry is action, a recording of movement and thought.

Book of Exercises II initially followed the same pattern: Seferis began organizing and completing unfinished writing projects upon his return to Greece from his final post as ambassador to the United Kingdom in 1962. In early 1963, Ikaros Press issued an advertisement for *Book of Exercises II*, which was to be made up of recent and previously unpublished work. Yet the manuscript was quickly shelved when Seferis became a definite contender for the Nobel, as its content might have been received adversely.

In December 1963, Seferis became the first Greek writer to receive the Nobel Prize for Literature. His Nobel lecture praised the "vulgar, popular, and oral tradition" across Greek culture, the "many generations of dedicated workers who sacrificed their lives to advance the spirit a little more." With the Nobel Prize, Seferis cemented his reputation as a servant to the nation, honoring its poetic tradition and geopolitical needs.

Just a few years later, the military coup of April 1967 and the right-wing, anti-communist Regime of the Colonels brought down the "wall" between George's two professional personae. He expressed his disgust for the dictatorship and publicly condemned it in a statement to the foreign press, stating that "this anomaly must cease." The dictatorship destroyed freedom of the press and civil liberties, preventing free expression. Meanwhile, Seferis, who suffered from serious health problems throughout the '60s, died in 1971 without completing *Book of Exercises II*. In 1976, fourteen years after it was begun, *Book of Exercises II* was finally published by editor George Savidis following Seferis's directions and drafts.

Only a few of the "final poems" from *Book of Exercises II* were included in the 1981 and 1995 revised English editions of George Seferis's *Collected Poems*, translated by Edmund Keeley and Philip Sherrard and first published in 1961. Keeley and Sherrard argued for including only those poems which had already been authorized for English translation, citing Seferis's own reservations about posthumously publishing a poet's remainders. Their rejection of *Book of Exercises II* has made it terra incognita for English-speaking readers until now.

The present edition follows the categorization and layout of the Greek original, developed by George Savidis. The section called "Excerpts from *Days 5* (1945–1951)" contains poems from Seferis's diaries during the period of the Greek Civil War and his posting to Ankara, Turkey (some of this material was published in *A Poet's Journal: Days of 1945–1951*, translated by Athan Anagnostopoulos in 1974). "Final Poems (1968–1971)" are the last poems that Seferis wrote, including most notably "The Cats of St. Nicholas" and "On the Aspalathus...," which rebuke the Colonels' dictatorship.

"Circumstantial Poems (1931–1971)" are poems drawn from diaries, notebooks, and letters, while "Calligraphies (1941–1942)" are drawings containing poems that Seferis made while in exile during World War II. His "Calligraphies" are inspired by the French tradition of the *calligramme*, poems in which the typographical or calligraphic form reflect the content. Guillaume Apollinaire's *Poems of Peace and War, 1913–1916*, written during World War I are a well-known example and may have influenced Seferis. The Savidis edition also included four poems translated into Greek: an Edward Lear limerick, a quote from a Nahuatl traditional song, a Eugene McCarthy poem, and a Bashō haiku, which are not included here.

Book of Exercises II is more than a collection of the poet's remainders. It showcases Seferis's love of experimentation with form, tradition, humor, and personae beyond those from Greek myth. We hear the voices of his personal pseudonyms, of anthropomorphic figurines made out of nuts and twigs, of pompous blowhards, of supercilious British overlords, of complicit Greek politicians, of Byzantine cavalrymen, of lusty poets ancient and modern, plus horses, camels, and T. S. Eliot. *Book of Exercises II*'s array of characters and animals express emotions, opinions, and proclivities beyond the bounds of social convention and a diplomat's purported neutrality.

Here we see how Seferis relished both traditional and oral poetic forms, utilizing them to express disgust, offense, and desire. "Partisans in the Middle East," "Afternoon of a Faun," and "Chorale from *Matthew Paschalis, Prisoner of War*" use storytelling and musical rhymes to satirize the horrors of World War II and the ineptitudes of the Greek government in the face of enemies, allies, and internal factions. With similar devices, "Syngrou Avenue II" deftly plays with racial and colonial tropes to ridicule King George II's restoration by comparing Greece in 1935 to Ethiopia under Mussolini. "Indian Folktale" combines an enclosed rhyme scheme and Sanskrit words drawn from the *Mahabharata* for the sole purpose of telling critics to piss off. "What the Camel Said" is a lascivious send-up of T. S. Eliot, a poet who fascinated Seferis, as critics and scholars have often discussed. "Ode in Bastardized Verse à la Kalvos" imitates the early modern romantic poet Andreas Kalvos to tell some inside jokes.

The erotic poetry in *Book of Exercises II* is a welcome eruption of joy and vitality from a poet who is described in his Nobel biography as writing about "themes of alienation, wandering, and death." Seferis dresses his desire in suitable forms—ancient supplications to Aphrodite, *mantinades* (traditional rhyming couplets), and limericks (inspired by his time as ambassador to the United Kingdom). And this is only the material that Seferis authorized for publication; according to Savidis, he left out "four verses in limerick form"—too dirty for publication—"six *mantinades* with couplets, four without; a 64-verse pastiche with the title 'Arete and Erotokritos,'"presumably a parody of the sixteenth-century Cretan romance, and "a twelve-verse set of rhymes in the Cypriot mode called 'To an English Lady.'"

I can't claim to share George Seferis's love of traditional verse form and rhyme as a mode of self-expression and innovation. Yet translating *Book of Exercises II* was the best kind of workout: the kind where you volunteer to be humbled and invigorated. Where Seferis uses traditional forms and meter, I have created the same effect with the rhythm and rhyme in English, and in some cases meter. Some poems are mimetic, imitating specific writers (T. S. Eliot, Andreas Kalvos) and traditions (Classical Greek and Vedic), and I have attempted to reflect these styles in English. In Greek and in English, these poems are imbued with the spirit of innovation within traditional constraints.

Translation is always a process of making difficult choices in search of an elusive equilibrium between an original and a new work. As I made my way through semantic, phonetic, symbolic, and visual alternatives, I attempted to hold within me a consistent voice and personality. This voice is marked by my own: an anglophone woman of the twenty-first century.

With *Book of Exercises II,* I have attempted to revive engagement with a poet known for being dour, doctrinaire, and "difficult." The era when Seferis's translators decided to overlook his erotica and satire is long past. In the ongoing epoch of death and destruction unleashed by the World Wars, sensuality, sarcasm, and lament are enduring rebukes to dehumanizing massacres and reactionary national fantasies. Though Seferis dedicated his life to advancing Greek national interests through his writing, he also expressed his doubts, dilemmas, and alternative readings of Greek culture, history, and contemporary events.

This book makes available a significant body of Seferis's work previously unknown to English-language readers. May it stand against the erasure of time. May it remind us that questions of migration, identity, and belonging are perennial and universal, and that self-expression, especially humor, is an adaptive way to cope with trauma, violence, and grief.

Τετράδιο γυμνασμάτων, Β΄

Book of Exercises II

Ἀπὸ τὶς «Μέρες Ε΄» *(1945-1951)*

Excerpts from Days 5 *(1945–1951)*

Γυμνοπαιδία, Υ.Γ.

Γενάρης 1945

Ἡ θάλασσα ποὺ σὲ πῆρε μακριὰ
τόσο ἁπαλὴ σὰν τὸν κόρφο μητέρας
αὐτὴ τὸ ξέρει.

Ὅ,τι ρωτοῦσες σὰν ἤσουν παιδὶ
τέτοια ψελλίζουν τώρα οἱ γερόντοι·
φαντασίες γιὰ ἀνώφελα ἀντικείμενα
σὰν κλειδωμένες κασέλες πνιγμένων θαλασσινῶν.
Κοίταξε· φοβοῦνται τὸ φῶς τοῦ ἥλιου
φοβοῦνται νὰ ἰδοῦν·
παραμιλοῦν, δὲν ἔχουν ἄλλο.

Παιδιὰ μεγάλωσαν πεινώντας
ξεριζώνοντας δέντρα ἐρημώνοντας τὰ βουνά·
ἄλλα παιδιὰ ρωτοῦν καὶ σ' ἀποκρίνουνται
γιατί πῆγαν ἕνα βῆμα παρακάτω —
στὴν ἀνηφόρα; στὴν κατηφόρα;
δὲν ξέρω, τὸ ἴδιο κάνει·
κι ἔχουν ἀκόμη πολλὲς φωτιὲς
ν' ἀνάψουν γιὰ τ' Ἁι-Γιαννιοῦ τὸ πανηγύρι.

Ἔλεγα κάποτε, τὸ αἷμα
φέρνει τὸ αἷμα κι ἄλλο αἷμα —
τὸ πῆραν γιὰ παράσταση σαλτιμπάγκων,
ἄχρηστα παραμύθια.
Ψιθύριζα ἀκόμη, βαριὲς οἱ πέτρες
κι ἀσήκωτες οἱ μυλόπετρες
ποὺ ἄκουσες μιὰ βραδιὰ νὰ σταματοῦν
στὸ σύνορο τοῦ καιροῦ,
καὶ τραγικὰ τὰ νέα κορμιὰ ποὺ βούλιαξαν —
«Τριμμένα ροῦχα» λέγαν οἱ φαρμακοί.

Postscript to Gymnopaedia

January 1945

The sea that took you far away,
soft as a mother's breast,
it knows.

The things you questioned as a child
are now the mumblings of old men,
fantasies of useless objects,
the sealed trunks of drowned sailors.
Look—they fear the light of the sun.
They're afraid to see—
they babble, they have nothing else.

Some children grow up hungry
uprooting trees, devastating mountains;
others ask questions and get answers.
Why did they get one step ahead—
Up? Or down?
I don't know, it makes no difference.
Still, they have many fires
to light for the feast of St. John.

Once upon a time I said blood
brings blood and more blood.
They took it as the performance
of a buffoon, useless fairy tales.
Still, I would whisper,
stones are heavy
and the millstones are unliftable.
You heard them grinding to a halt
one night on the edge of time,
then, tragically, young bodies, drowned—

—Μὰ πῶς θὰ ντυθοῦμε στὴν παγωνιὰ
ὅταν δὲν ἔχουμε καινούργια;
Καὶ τί νὰ πεῖς στοὺς φίλους σου
σὰν ἔχουν πίκρα καὶ σωπαίνουν
καὶ τὰ περιπαθῆ τραγούδια τὰ γλεντοῦν
μόνο οἱ μεγάλες πόρνες;

Καὶ τοῦτο ἀκόμη· νὰ ξεχωρίσεις
μιὰ στιγμὴ ζωῆς, νὰ ξεχωρίσεις
τὸν ἄνεμο ποὺ κλονίζει τὰ τριαντάφυλλα
καὶ τὰ τριαντάφυλλα, στὸ μικρὸ περιβόλι
σὲ μιὰ φούχτα γῆς —
καὶ τοῦτο τὸ προσπάθησα, θά 'λεγα
ὄχι καθόλου σὰν εἶδος στοχασμοῦ
ἀλλὰ σὰν εἶδος ἀνάσας
δικῆς μου, δικῆς σας,
ἢ καλύτερα σὰν εἶδος μιᾶς φωνῆς·
ἄνεμος ἡ φωνὴ καὶ διαβαίνει.

Ἡ θάλασσα ποὺ σὲ πῆρε μακριὰ
καὶ σὲ ξανάφερε στὸ γνώριμο λιμάνι
χαρίζοντάς σου τὴ σιγὴ μπροστὰ στὴ σκάλα
τὴν ἀνεξάντλητη τοῦ μεσημεριοῦ,
ξέρει νὰ σοῦ ἐξηγήσει
τὴ Μεγάλη Παρασκευὴ καὶ τὸ Πάσχα.

"Worn-out rags," said the sorcerers.
But how will we dress in the cold
when we have nothing new?
And what will you say to your friends
when they are sorrowful and fall silent
and the passionate songs delight
only whores?

Still, this too I said: You should perceive
life's moments, you should discern
the wind shaking the roses
from the roses, in a tiny garden
no larger than a handful of earth.
This I tried to do, I would say,
not as the mind's recollection,
but as a matter of breathing,
for me, for you,
or better yet as a kind of voicing;
the wind is a passing voice.

The sea took you far away
and brought you back to the familiar port,
granting you the silence beyond the docks,
the boundless midday silence.
The sea knows how to teach you
the mysteries of Good Friday and Easter.

Τυφλὸς

Ὁ ὕπνος εἶναι βαρὺς τὰ πρωινὰ τοῦ Δεκέμβρη
μαῦρος σὰν τὰ νερὰ τοῦ Ἀχέροντα, χωρὶς ὄνειρα,
χωρὶς μνήμη, κι οὔτε ἕνα φυλλαράκι δάφνη.
Ὁ ξύπνος χαρακώνει τὴ λησμονιὰ σὰν τὸ μαστιγωμένο δέρμα
κι ἡ παραστρατημένη ψυχὴ ἀναδύεται κρατώντας
συντρίμμια ἀπὸ χθόνιες ζωγραφιές, ὀρχηστρὶς
μ' ἀνώφελες καστανιέτες, μὲ πόδια ποὺ τρεκλίζουν
μωλωπισμένες φτέρνες ἀπ' τὴ βαριὰ ποδοβολὴ
στὴν καταποντισμένη σύναξη ἐκειπέρα.

Ὁ ὕπνος εἶναι βαρὺς τὰ πρωινὰ τοῦ Δεκέμβρη.
Κι ὁ ἕνας Δεκέμβρης χειρότερος ἀπ' τὸν ἄλλον.
Τὸν ἕνα χρόνο ἡ Πάργα τὸν ἄλλο οἱ Συρακοῦσες·
κόκαλα τῶν προγόνων ξεχωσμένα, λατομεῖα
γεμάτα ἀνθρώπους ἐξαντλημένους, σακάτηδες, χωρὶς πνοὴ
καὶ τὸ αἷμα ἀγορασμένο καὶ τὸ αἷμα πουλημένο
καὶ τὸ αἷμα μοιρασμένο σὰν τὰ παιδιὰ τοῦ Οἰδίποδα
καὶ τὰ παιδιὰ τοῦ Οἰδίποδα νεκρά.

Ἄδειανοὶ δρόμοι, βλογιοκομμένα πρόσωπα σπιτιῶν
εἰκονολάτρες καὶ εἰκονομάχοι σφάζουνταν ὅλη νύχτα.
Παραθυρόφυλλα μανταλωμένα. Στὴν κάμαρα
τὸ λίγο φῶς χώνουνταν στὶς γωνιὲς
σὰν τὸ τυφλὸ περιστέρι.
Κι αὐτὸς
ψηλαφώντας βάδιζε
στὸ βαθὺ λιβάδι
κι ἔβλεπε σκοτάδι
πίσω ἀπὸ τὸ φῶς.

Δεκέμβρης 1945

The Blind Man

Sleep is heavy on December mornings,
black like the waters of the Acheron, without dreams,
without memory, without even a tiny laurel leaf.
Waking gouges oblivion like flogged skin
and the errant soul comes to the surface
holding shards of unearthed images, a dancing girl
with useless castanets, with feet that falter,
with ankles bruised from the heavy trampling
down where the annihilated gather.

Sleep is heavy on December mornings.
And each December is worse than the last.
One year it's Parga, the next it's Syracuse;
the ancestors' bones are exhumed, mines are
filled with exhausted souls, crippled, without breath,
and blood is bought and blood is sold,
spread around like the children of Oedipus,
and the children of Oedipus are dead.

Empty streets, pockmarked facades,
iconolaters and iconoclasts slaughter each other all night.
Latched shutters. Within the room
the scant light burrowed into corners
like a blind pigeon.
                                        And him—
groping, he found his way
through the vast meadow
and saw the darkness
behind the light.

December 1945

Ἀπρίλης

Κι ἂς ἦρθε ὁ Ἀπρίλης μὲ τὰ βάγια καὶ τὶς πασχαλιές·
πιὰ δὲν ἀκούω τίποτε, θαρρεῖς καὶ χιόνισε ὅλη νύχτα.

5.4.1946

April

Even though April has arrived with palms and lilacs,
I still don't hear anything. You would think it had snowed all night.

April 5, 1946

«Νότες» γιὰ ἕνα ποίημα

α΄

Ἑλικοβλέφαρη χαμογελούσα
βαθύζωνη μέσα στὴν τραγικὴ γαλήνη —

β΄

Κι ἂν τραγουδῶ ἀνάμεσα στὰ σκέλεθρα
καὶ στὶς ψυχὲς ποὺ σώσανε τὸ λάδι
μόνος στὸν ἔρημον αὐλόγυρο
ἑνὸς μοναστηριοῦ τῶν χρόνων τῆς τουρκοκρατίας
κοιτάζοντας ἀκίνητες καμπάνες ποὺ ὡριμάζουν —

γ΄

Μὲ τὸ κοντύλι μου ἔγραψα τὸ μυστικὸ κρεβάτι
κι ἦταν τριγύρω τ' ἀναμμένα βάτα ποὺ ἔγλειφαν τὰ μέλη
ἴσκιοι φιδιῶν τυλίγανε τὰ μελαψὰ λαγόνια
καὶ στῆς κοιλιᾶς τὴ λίμνη κολυμποῦσε κόκκινο ἕνα χέλι —

δ΄

Σύντροφοι ποὺ χορεύετε μασκαρεμένοι
σὲ μιὰ κορφὴ ποὺ πάτησε τόσες φορὲς ὁ χαλασμὸς
παίζοντας μὲ χρωματιστὲς κορδέλες
χορεύοντας, κοιτάχτε, τὸ γαϊτανάκι —

ε΄

Κι ὁ γήλιος τρυπώντας τὶς φυλλωσιὲς
πετάει στὸ χῶμα χρυσὰ τσεκίνια
ἀπόκριση στὴν προσφορὰ τοῦ καθενός μας —

"Musical Notes" for a Poem

1
A woman with flashing eyes, smiling,
the sash of her dress hanging low,
standing amidst the tragic serenity—

2
Let me sing among skeletons
and souls whose light faded
alone on the deserted courtyard wall
of a monastery from the time of the Ottoman Empire,
while watching motionless bells ripen—

3
I traced a mystic orgy in chalk,
it was surrounded by burning bushes that licked the members,
shadowy snakes encircled the dark-skinned loins,
and in the belly's lake a red eel swam—

4
Oh friends, how you dance, masked,
on a mountaintop stamped by throngs,
playing with colorful ribbons,
dancing, look, there's the maypole—

5
And the sun punctures the greenery,
casts golden doubloons on the ground
a response to our self-offering—

στ΄

Ὅπως τὰ ζαρωμένα πρόσωπα γερόντων
πέφτουν σὰν προσωπίδες σ᾽ ἀνοιγμένους λάκκους —

ζ΄

Ἡ ἀγάπη τὸ γαληνεμένο σπίτι τοῦ ἀνθρώπου.
(ΜΕΓΚ ΤΣΟΥ, 17)

η΄

Ὁ σταυραϊτὸς ἐδάγκωσε μιὰ ρώγα κι ἄλλη ρώγα
καὶ κάρφωσε τὰ νύχια του στὴν ἄγονη κοιλιὰ
κι εἶδα μέσ᾽ ἀπ᾽ τὰ σύννεφα νὰ χύνεται μιὰ φλόγα
ποὺ ἔσβησε μὲ τὸ ματωμένο κύμα στὴν ἀκρογιαλιά.

θ΄

Ἀντάρης: τὸ βυσσινὶ σκυλόδοντο τῆς Ἀφροδίτης.

ι΄

Ἄδεια πελάγη, ἄδεια καράβια, κεφάλια ἀδύναμα,
ψυχὲς πιασμένες στὸ δίχτυ τῆς μεγάλης ἀράχνης —

ια΄

Καὶ τὴν ἄκουσες τὴν αὐγὴ νὰ οὐρλιάζει·
«Θυμήσου τὰ λουτρὰ ποὺ σὲ θανάτωσαν, πατέρα»,
ὄχι μονάχα στὴν κυψέλη τῶν θησαυρισμένων τάφων
ἀλλὰ κι ἐδῶ στὶς γειτονιὲς μὲ τοὺς ἀκοίμητους
κινηματογράφους,
στὸ περιβόλι τῆς πολιτείας ποὺ τὸ κατάπιε ἡ νύχτα,
στὸ Σύνταγμα μπροστὰ στὸν Ἄγνωστο Στρατιώτη:
Πόσα λεπτὰ σιωπῆς κοστίζει μιὰ ζωή;
«Θυμήσου τὰ λουτρὰ ποὺ σὲ θανάτωσαν, πατέρα»·
μονάχα τὸ αἷμα θὰ ποτίζει τὴ ζωὴ καὶ τ᾽ ἀηδόνι,
ἔτσι ὅπως τραγουδᾶ τὸν πόθο του πίσω ἀπ᾽ τὶς κλειδωμένες
γρίλιες

6
The wizened faces of old men
fall into open graves
like masks—

7
Love, man's serene home.
(Mencius, pg. 17)

8
The eagle bit a nipple and then one again,
dug its talons into the barren abdomen,
from the clouds I saw a flame descend,
a bloodied wave brought it to an end.

9
Antares: the cherry-red dogtooth of Venus.

10
Empty sea, empty boats, weak minds,
souls caught in the net of the great spider—

11
And you heard her howling at dawn:
"Remember the baths where they murdered you, father,"
not only in the ancient beehive-shaped tombs and treasuries,
but here, too, in the neighborhoods with sleepless movie theaters,
in the city garden swallowed by night,
in Syntagma before the Tomb of the Unknown Soldier.
How many moments of silence does one life cost?
"Remember the baths where they murdered you, father."
Blood alone will nourish life
and the nightingale.
He sings of his desire, caged,

(ἀφηρημένος, σκυμμένο τὸ κεφάλι περνάει στὸ δρόμο
ἕνας καταδικασμένος σὲ θάνατο ἀπὸ ὅλους)
γιὰ τὰ παιδάκια ποὺ αὔριο θὰ 'ρθοῦν νὰ παίξουν μὲ
καινούργιες κουδουνίστρες —

ιβ΄
Ἢ χρώματα σὲ φορεσιὲς θεατρίνων ποὺ μόλις θυμόμαστε
κάποτε λάμπουν —

ιγ΄
Περνῶ μπροστὰ σὲ εἰκόνες ποὺ χαλνῶ·
τὸ μεγάλο εἰκονοστάσι —

ιδ΄
Σκαρφαλώνοντας λέξεις ὅπως μιὰν ἀνεμόσκαλα.

Μάης – Ἰούνιος 1946

(lost in thought, head bowed, a man condemned to death
  by all passes on the street)
in the name of tomorrow's children
who will come and play with new rattles—

12
Or colors of actors' robes, we barely remember them,
they were illuminated once—

13
I pass in front of icons that I destroy;
the great iconostasis—

14
Scrambling up words as if they were a rope ladder.

May–June 1946

Μεροληψία

Μὲ μάτια ποὺ ἔβλεπαν
ὄχι τὸ σῶμα ἀλλὰ τὶς φλέβες
μὲ φλέβες ποὺ ἄγγιζαν
ὄχι τὴ σάρκα ἀλλὰ τὰ νεῦρα
μὲ νεῦρα ποὺ ἔσμιγαν
ὄχι τὰ χείλια ἀλλὰ τὰ δόντια
μὲ δόντια ποὺ δάγκωναν τὴν κοιλιά·
μὲ κοιλιὰ ποὺ δέχουνταν τὴ φρίκη
ὄχι τὸ σπέρμα
κι ἡ φρίκη φούσκωνε τὰ βυζιὰ
καὶ τὰ βυζαῖναν οἱ ζητιάνοι:
ἥσυχη ὡραία καὶ ἀπαλή,
περίμενε τὴν ἄλλη μέρα
τὸν ἄλλο μήνα τὸν ἄλλο χρόνο
ἀνάμεσό μας, ἐκστατική.

12.7.1946

Partisanship

The eyes perceived
not a body but the veins within,
the veins met
not just flesh but nerves,
the nerves merged into
teeth rather than lips,
the teeth bit into the womb;
as soon as the womb took on the monstrosity
rather than sperm,
the breasts swelled in horror
and nursed beggars:
silent, lovely, and gentle,
it waited for the next day,
the next month, the next year
among us, in ecstasy.

July 12, 1946

Οἱ μέρες εἶναι πέτρες. Τσακμακόπετρες
ποὺ ἔτυχε νά 'βρει ἡ μιὰ τὴν ἄλλη κι ἔγιναν δυὸ-τρεῖς σπίθες·
πέτρες τοῦ ἀλωνιοῦ ποὺ τὶς χτυποῦν τὰ πέταλα κι ἔλιωσαν
πολὺ κόσμο,
βότσαλα στὸ νερὸ μὲ τὰ ἐφήμερα δαχτυλίδια,
πετραδάκια πολύχρωμα καὶ ὑγρὰ στ' ἀκρογιάλι,
ἢ λήκυθοι, στῆλες ποὺ κάποτε σταματοῦν τὸ διαβάτη.
Οἱ μέρες εἶναι πέτρες· σωριάζουνται ἡ μιὰ πάνω στὴν ἄλλη...

8.10.1946

These days are like stones. Flint stones
that happened to find one another and created two or three
sparks;
stones on the threshing floor pounded by hooves, obliterating
many souls;
rocks in the sea touched by momentary rings;
tiny multicolored pebbles wet on the shore;
or funerary urns—headstones that sometimes draw the attention
of a passerby.
These days are like stones. They pile up, one on top of the other...

October 8, 1946

Ὁ ἄνθρωπος ποὺ τοῦ ’κλεψαν τὸν ἴσκιο

Θὰ σοῦ πάρουν τὸν ἴσκιο τῶν δέντρων, θὰ τὸν πάρουν
θὰ σοῦ πάρουν τὸν ἴσκιο τῆς θάλασσας, θὰ τὸν πάρουν
θὰ σοῦ πάρουν τὸν ἴσκιο τῆς καρδιᾶς, θὰ τὸν πάρουν
θὰ πάρουν τὸν ἴσκιο σου...

15.3.1947

The Man Whose Soul Was Stolen

They'll take the soul of the trees from you, they'll take it.
They'll take the soul of the sea from you, they'll take it.
They'll take your heart's soul, they'll take it,
they'll take your soul...

March 15, 1947

Οἰδιπόδειο, '48

Ὁ Σέρλοκ Χὸλμς ἔχει ὑποκαταστήματα παντοῦ
σ' ὅλη τὴ γῆ, σ' ὅλη τὴν οἰκουμένη·
ὁ Οἰδίπους ἀνακρίνει τὸ βοσκὸ παντοῦ
χωρὶς νὰ ξέρει τί τὸν περιμένει.

Παραφυλάει στὸ σταυροδρόμι ὁ Λάιος ὁ νεκρὸς
καὶ στὰ περβόλια ἀκοῦς τραυλίσματα: «τυφλὸς τά τ' ὦτα...»
μὲ χαλασμένο φρένο, νευρικός, τρέχει ὁ καιρὸς —
Κύριος! ἐδῶ σβήνουν τὰ μάτια καὶ τὰ φῶτα!

Ἄγκυρα, 8.10.1948

Oedipus Complex, '48

Sherlock Holmes has franchises everywhere
across the earth and the civilized world.
Oedipus interrogates the shepherd everywhere
without knowing what awaits him.

At the crossroads, dead Laius keeps watch.
The voice wailing *your eyes are blind* reaches every yard.
Time runs on with faulty brakes, anxiously—
Sir! This is where all eyes and lights are extinguished!

Ankara, October 8, 1948

«Ἀργώ»

Τὰ παραμύθια μου τά 'μαθα κοντὰ στὰ καράβια
ὄχι ἀπὸ ταξιδιῶτες μήτε ἀπὸ θαλασσινοὺς
μήτε ἀπ' τοὺς ἄλλους ποὺ προσμένουν στὰ μουράγια
παντοτινὰ ξέμπαρκοι ψάχνοντας τὶς τσέπες τους γιὰ τσιγάρο.
Πρόσωπα καραβιῶν κατοικοῦν τὴ ζωή μου·
ἄλλα κοιτάζουν μ' ἕνα μάτι σὰν τὸν Κύκλωπα
ἀκίνητα στοῦ πελάγου τὸν καθρέφτη
ἄλλα προχωροῦν σὰν ὑπνοβάτες, ἐπικίνδυνα
κι ἄλλα τὰ πῆρε ὁ ὕπνος τοῦ βυθοῦ
ξύλα σκοινιὰ καραβόπανα κι ἀλυσίδες.
Στὸ δροσερὸ σπιτάκι τοῦ περιβολιοῦ
ἀνάμεσα στὰ καβάκια καὶ τοὺς εὐκάλυπτους
κοντὰ στὸ σκουριασμένον ἀνεμόμυλο
κοντὰ στὴν κίτρινη δεξαμενὴ μ' ἕνα χρυσόψαρο μονάχα
στὸ δροσερὸ σπιτάκι μυρίζοντας λυγαριὰ
βρῆκα ἕνα μπούσουλα καραβίσιο
αὐτὸς μοῦ 'δειξε τοὺς ἀγγέλους τῶν καιρῶν
ποὺ κατοικοῦν τὴν καταμεσήμερη σιγή.

Νοέμβρης 1948

Argo

I learned my fables among boats,
not from travelers nor from mariners,
nor from the others who waited on the quays,
disembarked, perpetually searching their pockets for a cigarette.
The faces of boats inhabit my life—
some of them see with one eye, like the Cyclops,
motionless upon the sea's mirror,
others move like sleepwalkers, dangerously.
Still others were taken by the sleep of the deep
wood, ropes, sails, chains, and all.
In the cool little garden house,
among the cottonwood and eucalyptus trees,
close to the rusty windmill,
close to the yellow fountain with one lonely carp,
in the cool little house with the aroma of reeds,
I found a boat's compass.
It revealed the atmospheric angels
who occupy the noonday silence.

November 1948

Τὸ χιόνι ἐδῶ δὲν τελειώνει. Στὴν Ἀττικὴ
τὸ δέχουνται σὰν ἕνα διάλειμμα ποὺ ξεκουράζει
ἢ μιὰ κατάνυξη ποὺ προμηνᾶ τὶς ἀνθισμένες μυγδαλιὲς
ἢ τὸ σεντόνι τοῦ Καραγκιόζη σὰν πάψουν οἱ κλαπαδόρες.
Χαίρεται ὁ κόσμος· βγαίνει στὶς ἐξοχὲς καὶ λησμονᾶ
τὴ φτώχεια. Τὸ χιόνι ἐδῶ
εἶναι τὸ μηδέν. Μίλια κάτω ἀπὸ τὸ μηδὲν
μὲ τὴ μαρμαρυγὴ τῆς ἄσπρης ἄμμου, πρόσωπα
χωρὶς μάγουλα, χωρὶς μορφή, μάτια
παραμονεύουν χωρὶς τὸ εὐλογημένο χῶμα.
Δὲ θὰ τολμοῦσα νὰ μιλήσω γιὰ προσευχές, κι ὅμως
κάποτε σφάζουν ἕνα ἀρνὶ γιὰ τὶς θυσίες·
τὸ αἷμα ξεσπᾶ σὰν ἔκρηξη ἥλιου τυφλωτική.

Στιγμὲς ποὺ φεύγουν ὅλα, κι ὁ κάθε κρότος
μοιάζει πρωτάκουστος· πέφτει θαρρεῖς
σὲ μιὰ παλάμη ἀπὸ πέτρα ἢ ξύλο.
Καὶ πᾶνε οἱ ἄνθρωποι γεννώντας ἀγάλματα.

Γενάρης 1949

The snow here never ends. In Attica
the snow is welcomed as a refreshing pause,
or a holy sign, anticipating the almond blossoms,
or the scrim for the shadows of Karagöz puppets when the
    noisemakers have ceased.
Everyone rejoices; they go to the countryside to forget
their poverty. But here the snow
nullifies, a nothingness with the shimmer of white sand.
Miles below, beyond the blessed earth, lurk faces
without cheeks, without form, only eyes.
I would never dare to speak of prayers, and yet
sometimes they slaughter a lamb for their sacrifices;
the blood bursts forth like a blinding eruption of sun.

These are moments when everything disappears and each crack
seems to be heard for the first time, a sound like
striking an open palm made of stone or wood.
And people go on, giving birth to lifeless figures.

January 1949

Μὲ λαμπυρίσματα γυαλιοῦ, μὲ τὴ σιγὴ τραγουδοῦσε τὸ χιόνι.
Σκοτώνει τούτη ἡ μουσική· μέρες χαθῆκαν τὰ σπουργίτια·
  πᾶνε νὰ θάψουν τοὺς νεκρούς των.
Κι οἱ σταλαχτίτες ἀπὸ τὰ δέντρα χτυπᾶνε τὴ γκρινιάρικη χορδὴ
  τοῦ ξεθυμασμένου ἥλιου.
Ἀφῆστε με ν' ἀκούσω τὸν ἀδερφό μου —

27.3.1949

The snow sang with a glassy radiance, in silence.
This music kills; the sparrows have been missing for days.
They've gone to bury their dead.
And stalactites from trees strike the grumpy chords of the
dying sun.
Leave me alone so I can listen to my brother—

March 27, 1949

Canzona

Μορφὴ τῶν βυθισμένων Ἁγιασμάτων
μάνα τῆς ἄγνοιας καὶ τῆς σοφίας
μάνα τῆς μάχης καὶ τῆς εἰρήνης
μάνα στὴ χώρα τῶν ζωντανῶν,

κοντὰ σὲ βρύσες τραγουδιστὲς
ὅπου λυθῆκαν τὰ νερὰ
κοντὰ στὸν ἦχο τοῦ ἀργαλειοῦ,
κι ὅπου τὸ χιόνι δὲν τελειώνει
κι ὅταν θλιβόμαστε κι ὅταν χαιρόμαστε
γιὰ τὰ σπουδαῖα καὶ γιὰ τὴν κολοκύθα,
βοήθησέ μας.

Πάνω ἀπ' τὴ φωτεινὴ κατήφεια τῆς ἐρήμου
κι ἀνάμεσα στὰ ἔθνη ποὺ μᾶς ἀγαποῦν
ἢ μᾶς ἐχτρεύουνται ἢ μᾶς παραγνωρίζουν·
σὲ πολιτεῖες ποὺ στράγγισαν μὲς στὰ τειχιά τους·
κάτω στοὺς κάμπους τῶν πολεμίων,
στάσου κοντά μας.

Κι ἀνάμεσα στ' ἀδέρφια μας ποὺ κλώθουν
στὶς φλέβες τους τὸ δίκλωνο αἷμα,
στὸν ἄγριο φόβο τῆς ἀγάπης
στὴν τρυφερότητα τοῦ μίσους
στὴν κατηφόρα τοῦ σκοταδιοῦ,
βοήθησέ μας.

Δῶσε μας ἕναν ὕπνο μὲ ὄνειρα
σὰν τὸ κουπί μας, σὰν ἐκεῖνα

Canzona

You, submerged in sacred depths,
in the form of Holy Grace,
Mother of ignorance and wisdom,
Mother of strife and peace,
Mother in the land of the living,

near singing taps
where waters course,
near the sound of the loom
and where the snow doesn't end
and when we're grieving and when we're happy
about what matters and what doesn't,
help us.

Above the shining gloom of the wasteland,
and among the nations who love us
or those who make us enemies or who misunderstand us,
in cities where the walls squeeze souls,
in the battlefields beyond,
stand by us.

You who are within our brothers,
the ones spinning double-stranded blood in their veins,
in the wild fear of love,
in the tenderness of hatred,
in the descent of darkness,
help us.

Grant us sleep with dreams
like oars, the ones we have

ποὺ ἔχουμε κεντημένα στὸ πετσί μας
μὲ πελαγίσια ὑπομονή·
ὄχι τὸν κυβιστὴ τὸν Ἐφιάλτη.

Προύσα, Μάης 1949

embroidered on our skin
with oceanic patience,
instead of the cubist nightmare.

Prousa, May 1949

«L'angolo francescano»

Ἀνάμεσα στὶς μέρες τοῦ κερασιοῦ καὶ τὶς μέρες τοῦ βύσσινου,
ὅταν ἀρχίζουν τὰ βερίκοκα νὰ γίνουνται
καὶ δὲν ἀκοῦς νὰ πέφτουνε τὰ μῆλα,
τὸ μικρὸ περιβόλι χωρὶς ὁρίζοντα
κι οἱ φυλλωσιὲς δίνουν τὰ χέρια ὁλοῦθε καὶ σὲ κλείνουν.
Ἀνάμεσα σὲ τοῦτα τὰ βουνὰ μὲ χρῶμα πέρα ἀπ' τὴ ζωὴ
σ' αὐτὲς τὶς ἐρημιές, στεγνοὺς βυθοὺς
ἀπὸ πελάγη ποὺ ἄλλοτε θὰ νά 'χες ἀρμενίσει,
στὸ μικρὸ περιβόλι, νά οἱ καρποὶ
νά τὰ παιδιὰ τῆς θρησκείας·
ἄγουρες προσφορὲς ὥριμες προσφορές, προσφορὲς σάπιες.
—Πῶς γίναμε ἔτσι;
Ρώτα καλύτερα
τοὺς ἐπωδοὺς τοὺς μάγους καὶ τοὺς φαρμακούς,
γιὰ μένα φτάνει
νὰ βλέπω αὐτὴ τὴ φυλλωσιά, τοῦτο τὸ σῶμα·
ἄγουρες γωνιὲς ὥριμες γωνιές, γωνιὲς χτυπημένες.
Τὰ κεράσια πέρασαν τὰ μῆλα θ' ἀργήσουν ἀκόμη
καὶ τὸ φεγγάρι μὲ θολωτὰ φτερὰ περιστεριοῦ
στὰ λινὰ ντυμένο
καθὼς ἀκούω στὴ μικρὴ δεξαμενὴ τὴν ἀκατάπαυτη στάλα,
κομπολόι μαθητευόμενου, χάντρες ἀπὸ φτωχὸ πανηγύρι —
κι ἡ πόρνη κρατώντας τσακισμένο γυαλὶ τὰ μύρα
κάτω στὶς ἰτιὲς τῶν Σοδόμων.

1.8.1949

"L'Angolo Franciscano"

Between the time of the sweet cherries and the sour,
the apricots begin to ripen
and you can't hear the apples falling;
the little orchard lacks a horizon
and the foliage extends its hands from all sides and encloses you.
Between those mountains of a lifeless color
and these deserts, dry depths.
In the distance between the sea you once sailed
and this little garden, here are the fruits,
here are the children of faith:
unripe offerings, ripe offerings, rotten offerings.
—How did we turn out this way?
                                        Better ask
the enchanters, the sorcerers, the alchemists.
For me it's enough
to look at this foliage, this body,
unripe corners, ripe corners, corners bruised.
The cherries have passed, the apples will come later,
the moon too, dressed in linen
the color of a dove's murky wings.
I'm listening to the unceasing trickle of the small cistern—
it's a student's worry beads, the evil-eye charms from a meager
    religious feast;
it's a prostitute holding a ragged vial of myrrh oil
under the willows of Sodom.

August 1, 1949

Άγκυρανὸ μνημεῖο

Κάθε τὸ μήνα μιὰ φορὰ κάθε τρεῖς ἑβδομάδες
μαντατοφόροι ν-ἔρχουνται μαντατοφόροι φεύγουν.
Ποιὰ προσταγὴ τοὺς ἔστειλε κανένας δὲν τὸ ξέρει·
μήτε οἱ γερόντοι ποὺ ἔχουνε κόκαλο ἀπὸ λελέκι
μήτε οἱ κοπέλες ποὺ ἔχουνε στὰ φρύδια χελιδόνα
καὶ μήτε τὰ στεγνὰ βουνὰ μὲς στὴ Γαλλογραικία.
Ἔρχουνται ἀπ' τὴν Ἀνατολὴ κι ἔρχουνται ἀπὸ τὴ Δύση
ἀπὸ Βοριὰ κι ἀπὸ Νοτιά, τριαντάφυλλο τοῦ ἀγέρα.
Ἀφήνουν τ' ἄτια ρέμπελα καὶ τρέχουν νὰ μεθύσουν
κι ἀπ' τὶς ταβέρνες βγαίνουνε τρεκλίζοντας καὶ πᾶνε
παραμιλώντας ἄμοιαστα, τρελοὶ κι ὀνειρεμένοι.
Ἕνας λέει γιὰ τὸν Αὔγουστο πού 'χε γιὰ λέπια κάστρα,
ἄλλος γυρεύει Παναγιὲς ποὺ ρέψανε στὰ σπήλαια
κι ἕνας χαμηλοκούτελος τὸ βασιλιὰ Ἀσιτάουντα
πού 'χε πατέρα δρόλαπα καὶ μάνα τὴ φουρτούνα
καὶ τώρα ἀπόμεινε ἄλαλος σὰν τὸ ξερὸ ποτάμι.
Μὰ ὁ Στάθης ὁ καλόγερος πὄσωσε περπατώντας
κι ἦταν σπαθάρης μιὰ φορά, σπαθάρης καὶ τζελάτης,
στὸ σιντριβάνι κάθεται, νερὸ τὸ τυφλοφόρο,
κοιτάζει τὸ βασίλεμα καὶ λέει κι ἀπολογᾶται:
«Στὸν κάτω κόσμο μ' ἔστειλες, Ἀφέντη καὶ Χριστέ μου,
κι ὁλάκερος ἐμίσεψα κι ὁλάκερος ἐπῆγα·
τώρα τὴ χάρη σου ζητῶ, τῆς ἁμαρτίας δραγάτη·
σπόρο τοῦ χάρου ν-ἔσπειρα, νὰ τὸν θερίσουν ἄλλοι
καὶ κάνε ἀπὸ τὸν τάφο μου γιὰ σένα νὰ βλαστήσω,
γαρίφαλο τοῦ θρήνου μου καὶ στὸ πλευρό σου νά 'ρθω».

5.8.1949

Monumentum Ancyranum

Once a month, or maybe it's once every three weeks,
messengers come and messengers go.
No one knows at whose behest they were sent—
neither the old men who have stork-like bones
nor the young women who have swallow-shaped eyebrows.
And the dry mountains of Anatolian Galatia don't know either.
They come from the East and they come from the West,
from the North and the South,
from every direction on the compass rose.
Their horses roam free while they rush to get drunk.
They stagger out of taverns and wander,
babbling strangely, crazed and dreamy.
One says that Augustus had a castle made of fish scales,
another goes after Holy Virgins who expired in caves,
and one Hamilokoutelos seeks the Hittite king Azatiwata,
who is speechless now like a dried-up river,
though his father was a cyclone and his mother a gale.
But Stathis, the monk who was saved while on campaign
and once was a lieutenant, an aide-de-camp, and executioner,
this Stathis sits on the fountain with blinding water,
watches the sunset and speaks, pleading:
"You sent me to the underworld, my Lord and Christ,
and always I took my leave and went.
Now I, sin's field marshal, seek your favor.
I sowed seeds of death, so that others could reap them.
Make me blossom from my tomb for thee,
Carnation of my lament, may I flank thee."

August 5, 1949

Ἐπιτύμβιο στὴ γάτα μου τὴν Τούτη ποὺ μᾶς ἄφησε χρόνους τὸ περασμένο φθινόπωρο

Εἶχε τὸ χρῶμα τοῦ ἔβενου τὰ μάτια τῆς Σαλώμης
ἡ Τούτη ἡ γάτα ποὺ ἔχασα· διαβάτη, μὴ σταθεῖς.
Βγῆκε ἀπ' τὸ χάσμα ποὺ ἔκοβε στῆς μέρας τὸ σεντόνι
τώρα νὰ σκίσει δὲν μπορεῖ τοῦ ζόφου τὸ πανί.

Ἄγκυρα, 22.8.1949

Epitaph for My Cat Named This One Who Left Us Years Ago Last Fall

This One, the cat I lost,
was the color of ebony with the eyes of Salome.
Passerby, don't pause.
She sliced a chasm in daylight's sheet and emerged.
Now she can't shred the veil of Hades's gloom.

Ankara, August 22, 1949

Ἦταν καλὸ τὸ χοιροστάσι·
πέρ' ἀπ' τὴ λάσπη τίποτε
σὰν τ' ὄνειρο τὸ χαμηλὸ
στὴ βαθιὰ κοίτη·
τίποτε παρακάτω
κι ὁ θάνατος περίπου σὰν τὸ δικό σας
χωρὶς μελέτη —

Νοέμβρης 1949

It was a good slaughterhouse,
nothing beyond mud,
a low-lying dream
at vision's depth.
Nothing beyond that
and death was more or less
like all of yours—
unexamined.

November 1949

«Φιλοκτήτης»

Τραυματισμένο κορμί, τραυματισμένος ὁ τόπος,
τραυματισμένος ὁ καιρὸς —

Νοέμβρης 1949

Philoctetes

A wounded body. The country is wounded.
A time of wounding—

November 1949

Βγήκαμε ἀπὸ τὰ τείχη — ποιὸς μᾶς τρόμαζε;
Ἔξω κανείς· στὸ χῶμα χρώματα μαβιά, μαβιὰ πουλιά.
Κάποτε μεγάλοι βράχοι λάμποντας σὰν τοὺς καθρέφτες
κι ὁ ἄγγελος μὲ τὰ χρυσὰ τακούνια
ντύθηκε τὴ γύμνια του μ' ἕνα γαλάζιο φτερούγισμα —

22.6.1950

We emerged from the walls—who frightened us?
No one was there, just purple colors in the earth, purple birds.
Once upon a time there were rock faces gleaming like mirrors
and an angel with gold sandals
who wrapped his nakedness in a cerulean wingspan—

June 22, 1950

Γραμμένο μὲ τὸ μολύβι

Χωρὶς χιτώνα χωρὶς χείλια χωρὶς μάτια
μικροὶ βασιλιάδες μὲ τοὺς ἑταίρους καὶ τὶς παλλακὲς
κι ὅ,τι ξεφόρτωσε τὸ κρητικὸ καράβι
κάτω στὸ γιαλὸ στὴν Ἁλικαρνασσό·
ὀρθόστηθες σκλάβες ποὺ τὶς δασκάλεψαν τὰ φίδια
καὶ στενοὶ ἀκροβάτες ποὺ τοὺς δασκάλεψε ὁ ταῦρος
τόση πραμάτεια
κι ἔμποροι μὲ τοὺς λογαριασμοὺς τοῦ Λαβύρινθου.
Χωρὶς χιτώνα χωρὶς χείλια χωρὶς μάτια
ὅλοι γυρεύουνε νὰ ξεντυθοῦν τὸ χῶμα,
τ' ἀποζητοῦν
ἀκόμη κι ἀπὸ τοῦτες τὶς πλαγιὲς
π' ἀνοίγουν τόσους κόρφους στὸ φεγγάρι,
κι αὐτὸν τὸν ἄνθρωπο π' ἀκούμπησε νὰ ξαποστάσει
στῶν ἐπιγόνων τὴν κολόνα ἀκούγοντας
μὲ κλειστὰ βλέφαρα, τριζόνια καὶ βατράχια
νὰ σκάβουν.

Λάβρανδα, 27.6.1950

Written in Pencil

No chiton, no lips, no eyes.
Minor sovereigns with their retinues and courtesans
and whatever else was unloaded from the Cretan ship
below, on the beach in Halicarnassus.
Female slaves bound at their breasts
guided by snakes and thin acrobats led by a bull.
So much merchandise
and merchants with their labyrinthine accounts.
No chiton, no lips, no eyes.
They all sought to denude the earth,
they yearned for it.
Even taking from these sloping hills
that open into gulf after gulf
under the moonlight.
They open this man too,
leaning on our ancestors' column to recharge,
listening with closed eyes
to insects and frogs
digging.

Labraunda, June 27, 1950

Salva nos vigilantes

Μπουντρούμι

Τέτοιος οὐρανὸς γλυκὸς οὐρανὸς καὶ στὰ τειχιὰ
σμιλεμένα κρίνα σκουτάρια λιοντάρια καὶ
SALVA NOS DOMINE VIGILANTES
CUSTODI NOS DORMIENTES
στ' ἀνώφλι τῆς μεγάλης πόρτας.
Στὴν αὐλὴ τοῦ κάστρου
κόκκινα ἀπόκοτα λουλούδια,
τὰ λένε τώρα ψάρια φαρμακερά.
Ὁ ἄγγελος ἔφυγε δείχνοντας φτέρνες χρυσές,
φτέρνες καὶ στήθια τὸ χρῶμα τῆς χρυσόπετρας.
Κι ὁ πολιορκημένος ἄνθρωπος, μόνος, περίκλειστος·
δίψα· τὸ καστέλι ἀμπαρωμένο.
Κακόμοιρα κορμιὰ κι οἱ λόγχες στενεύουν τῶν πολεμίων
κι ἡ ἀγρύπνια.
Κάτω στὴν Ἀλικαρνασσό...
«Νὰ φίλουν τὸ λαιμό σου
καὶ νά 'σταζε ὁ ἱδρώτας μου στὶς ρῶγες τῶ βυζιῶ σου»...
Ἦταν παραμονὴ τοῦ Δώδεκα Ἀποστόλου
ποὺ χύθηκαν στὴν ἄμμο τὰ γαρίφαλά της,
κι ἐκείνη λυγμοὶ ὅλη νύχτα
κολυμπώντας σὲ ρηχοὺς καημούς·
τὴν ἄκουγε μπερδεμένος στὰ περίπλοκα στολίσματά της
σὰ μονομάχος τοῦ τσίρκου στὸ δίχτυ·
χέρια ξαγριεμένα.
Τέτοιος οὐρανὸς
καὶ τὸ μπακιρένιο φῶς τοῦ φεγγαριοῦ
στὸ περιβόλι μὲ τοὺς ὑπέρογκους κάκτους
τ' ὁλόγυμνο φεγγάρι
κι ἡ θάλασσα φτιαγμένη ἀπὸ δέρμα κι ἀνάσες.
Ψάρια φαρμακερὰ σὰν παραμύθι τοῦ Ἡρόδοτου,

Salva Nos Vigilantes

In Bodrum

What a sky, a sweet sky
and on the wall
chiseled lilies, shields, lions, and
SALVA NOS DOMINE VIGILANTES
CUSTODI NOS DORMIENTES
on the threshold of the great door.
On the castle's green
red wildflowers,
now they call them poisonous fish.
The angel departed, flashing his golden heels
and chest, the color of raw gold.
And the besieged man is alone, enclosed,
and thirsty but the castle is bolted shut.
Wretched bodies and warriors' spears draw closer,
with insomnia.
Below in Halicarnassus—
"Let them kiss your neck,
if only it were my sweat dripping onto your nipples... "
It was the eve of the feast of the Twelve Apostles
when her red carnations poured out on the sand,
and she sobbed all night,
swimming in shallow sorrows.
He heard her, tangled in her ornate gown
like a circus gladiator caught in a net,
hands enraged.
And the sky was like this—
the moon had a copper light
in the garden with the bulbous cacti,
a totally naked moon,
and the sea was formed from skin and breath.
Poisonous fish in the tale of Herodotus,

χρυσὲς φτέρνες, οἱ λόγχες λάμπουν στὸν ἥλιο·
SALVA NOS VIGILANTES —
                                                ὡς γιὰ τὸν ὕπνο
μιλοῦν γιὰ ἕνα περίτεχνο τάφο
πολὺ κοντά μας.

Ἰούλιος 1950

gold heels, the spears shining in the sun—
SAVE US, AWAKE—
                                        until it is the time
to speak of sleep,
of an ornate tomb,
quite near at hand.

July 1950

Ἔφεσος

Ὡστόσο σκύβουν
κάτω ἀπ' τὸ βῆμα τοῦ Θεοῦ
τὰ κυκλάμινα.

Ἄγκυρα, 30.10.1950

Ephesus

And still the cyclamens
bend beneath the footsteps
of God.

Ankara, October 30, 1950

Τελευταία ποιήματα (1968-1971)

Final Poems (1968–1971)

Γράμμα στὸν Rex Warner

πάροικο τοῦ Storrs, Connecticut, U.S.A. γιὰ τὰ ἐξήντα του χρόνια

Τὸν καιρὸ ποὺ συναντηθήκαμε
ἔλεγες τὸ κυνήγι τῆς ἀγριόχηνας
στὸ Δεσποτάτο τῶν ἑρμαφροδίτων·
ἐκεῖ τὸ γήπεδο τοῦ ποδόσφαιρου
εἶχε γνωρίσει τὴν ἀδιάντροπη σφαγή.
Γύριζα ἀπὸ ἕνα καλλιμάρμαρο στάδιο
ὅπου ὁ θεληματικὸς μαραθωνοδρόμος λαβωμένος
ἔβλεπε τὴ σφενδόνη ν' ἁρμενίζει στὸ αἷμα.
Ἔτσι σ' ἔνιωσα καὶ γίναμε φίλοι.

Πηγαίναμε σ' ἕναν τόπο ρημαγμένο ἀπὸ τὸν πόλεμο
ὥς καὶ τὶς κοῦκλες τῶν παιδιῶν τὶς εἶχαν σακατέψει.
Τὸ φῶς ταχὺ καὶ δυνατὸ
δάγκωνε κι ἀπολίθωνε τὰ πάντα.
Περπατούσαμε ἀνάμεσα
σὲ ποδήλατα καὶ χαρταετοὺς
βλέπαμε τὰ χρώματα μὰ ἡ κουβέντα μας
παραστρατοῦσε σ' ἐκείνη τὴν ἀνεπούλωτη φρίκη.

Πέρασαν χρόνια καὶ σὲ ξαναβρῆκα
στὰ χώματα μὲ τὴν πλούσια βλάστηση
ὅπου παραμονεύει κάποτε ὁ φαρμακερὸς κισσὸς
καὶ τὰ μελετηρὰ παιδιὰ μαθαίνουν
νὰ συλλαβίζουν τὰ σοφὰ βιβλία
καὶ τὸ λαβύρινθο τοῦ ἔρωτα.
Πάντα μνημόνευες τὸν Ὅμηρο καὶ τὴ γενιά του.
Σ' ἕνα τεράστιο δέντρο ὁ σκίουρος,
σπασμωδικὴ περισπωμένη, σκαρφάλωνε
ὁλοένα πιὸ ψηλὰ καὶ τὸν ἐκοίταζες
γελώντας.

Letter to Rex Warner

a resident alien of Storrs, Connecticut, USA, for his sixtieth birthday

When we met in the soccer field
that had experienced brazen slaughter
you were talking about hunting wild geese
in the Despotate of the Hermaphrodites.
I was returning from a marble stadium
where the wounded marathon runner
who volunteered for the war
saw slingshots sailing through blood.
This is how I attuned myself to you and we became friends.

We went to a country so badly
ruined by war that even the children's dolls were crippled.
The light was so quick and strong
it chewed through everything and turned it to bones.
We strolled among
bicycles and paper airplanes;
although we noticed the colors
our conversation strayed toward that unhealed terror.

Many years passed and I found you again
in soil teeming with flowers,
where sometimes the poison ivy lurks,
where studious young people learn
to pronounce scripture
and love's labyrinth.
You always honored Homer and his generation.
A squirrel scampered up a giant tree,
higher and higher, a spasming curlicue,
and you watched him, laughing.

Ζωή μας εἶναι πάντα ὁ ἀποχωρισμὸς
κι ἡ πιὸ δύσκολη παρουσία.

Τώρα σὲ ξανασυλλογίζομαι ἐδῶ
στὴν πολυπλόκαμη μητρόπολη.
Ὅλα τηλεόραση
δύσκολα 'γγίζεις κάτι ἀπὸ κοντά.
Μέσα στὴ ζέστη τῆς ἠλεχτρικῆς νύχτας
σὲ μιὰν ἀράγιστη μοναξιὰ βυθοῦ
οἱ φωταγωγημένοι οὐρανοξύστες
δείχνουν τὰ τζάμια τους γυαλιστερὰ
σὰν τὸ πετσὶ μεγάλου κήτους
καθὼς τινάχτηκε στὸν ἀφρό.
Ὁ πολύχρωμος λαὸς ποὺ τοὺς γέμιζε
ὁ ἄμετρος συνωστισμένος λαὸς
ἔφυγε τέτοιαν ὥρα
γι' ἄλλες χαρὲς καὶ γι' ἄλλα καρδιοχτύπια.
Τοὺς ἄδειασε, δὲν ἀπόμεινε ψυχὴ
σὰν τὶς φωλιὲς ἐκείνου τοῦ σπουργίτη
ποὺ ἐπονομάζεται φιλέταιρος
—Philetaerus Socius—, τὶς πολυκύτταρες·
τὶς βλέπεις στὴν ἀγκαθερὴ ἀκακία
ἢ στὸ μουσεῖο, ἂν τὶς γυρέψεις.
«Λελύπημαι ἐπὶ τῇ κολοκύνθῃ»
μουρμούριζε ὁ προφήτης Ἰωνὰς
κοιτάζοντας τὴ μεγάλη Νινευή.
Τοῦτος ὁ λόγος φέρνει τὸ μυαλὸ
σὲ ξυπνημένα ὀνείρατα ποὺ μάζεψε
στὸ μεροκάματό του:
Ταῦροι καὶ ἄλογα μ' ὀρθάνοιχτο στόμα
καὶ γλώσσα ξαφνικὸ πουνιάλο.
Ἕνας ἀπόδημος Θεοτοκόπουλος ὡσὰν τὸ βάραθρο τῆς ἀνάστασης
μιλώντας μιὰ λαλιὰ
ἀκατάληπτη γιὰ ὅλους.
Κι αὐτὸς ὁ γλύπτης

Our life is constant separation
and the most challenging presence.

Now, in the tightly woven metropolis,
I think of you again.
Everything is television and
it's hard to touch anything up close.
Within the heat of the electric night,
within a pristine loneliness of the sea's depths,
the illuminated skyscrapers
display their shiny windows
like the skin of a huge sea creature
as it flings itself into the foam.
The multicolored nation that fills the skyscrapers,
immeasurable, pushing and shoving,
departed about this time
for other pleasures and agonies.
They were emptied out, not a soul remained.
Like the nests of that sparrow,
the one dubbed a lover of company—
Philetairus socius—the multicellular ones.
You see them in thorny acacia shrubs
or in a museum, if you're looking for them.
"I rued the vine,"
murmured the prophet Jonah
while gazing at the great Nineveh.
This phrase reminds me of
ecstatic visions
that assembled in his daily work:
bulls and horses with gaping mouths
and a switchblade tongue.
The resurrection, a fissure in reality,
like the expat El Greco,
speaking in a tongue
unintelligible to all.
Or that sculptor

ποὺ ἔβλεπε κόκκινο τὸν οὐρανὸ
καὶ πάλευε μὲ τὸν ἀδηφάγο χῶρο
ποὺ γριτσάνιζε τὸ ἄγαλμα μέσα στὰ χέρια του
μικρὸ κι ἀκόμη πιὸ μικρὸ καὶ πιὸ λιγνὸ
ὢς τὸ τίποτε.
Βουλιάξανε βαθιὰ τὰ χρόνια ποὺ τὸ παλικάρι ὁ Μεγακλῆς
μὲ τὸ παγουράκι τοῦ ἀθλητῆ κρεμασμένο στὸ ζερβί του χέρι
κρατώντας στὰ τρία του δάχτυλα
ἕναν καρπὸ τῆς ροδιᾶς
πῆγε νὰ τὸν προσφέρει τρυφερὰ
στὴν Περσεφόνη.

Τώρα τὰ ἑξήντα σου καὶ δὲν μπορῶ
νὰ σοῦ χαρίσω τίποτε
παρὰ τοῦτο τ' ἀνώφελο τιτίβισμα.
Ὡστόσο λέω πὼς μ' ἔζωσαν καὶ μὲ παρακινοῦν
πυκνὸ κοπάδι τὰ φιλέταιρα σπουργίτια.

Νέα Ὑόρκη, N.Y., Ἰούνιος 1965 – Princeton, N.J., χειμώνας 1968

who saw the sky as red
and battled with that insatiable space
where the statue crumbled in his hands,
smaller and smaller and tinier
until nothing.
Many years have sunk into the depths since the time when
a young man named Megacles
had an athlete's flask draped on his left arm
and in his three fingers
held a pomegranate
and dedicated it tenderly
to Persephone.

Now, on your sixtieth, I can't
offer you anything
besides this useless twittering.
Nonetheless, I'll say that the company-loving sparrows
saved me and goaded me into their thick herd.

New York, NY, June 1965—Princeton, NJ, Winter 1968

Οἱ γάτες τ' Ἁι-Νικόλα

τὸν δ' ἄνευ λύρας ὅμως ὑμνῳδεῖ
θρῆνον Ἐρινύος
αὐτοδίδακτος ἔσωθεν
θυμός, οὐ τὸ πᾶν ἔχων
ἐλπίδος φίλον θράσος.
ΑΓΑΜΕΜΝΩΝ, 990 ἐπ.

«Φαίνεται ὁ Κάβο-Γάτα...», μοῦ εἶπε ὁ καπετάνιος
δείχνοντας ἕνα χαμηλὸ γιαλὸ μέσα στὸ πούσι
τ' ἄδειο ἀκρογιάλι ἀνήμερα Χριστούγεννα,
«...καὶ κατὰ τὸν Πουνέντε ἀλάργα τὸ κύμα γέννησε τὴν Ἀφροδίτη·
λένε τὸν τόπο Πέτρα τοῦ Ρωμιοῦ.
Τρία καρτίνια ἀριστερά!»
Εἶχε τὰ μάτια τῆς Σαλώμης ἡ γάτα ποὺ ἔχασα τὸν ἄλλο χρόνο
κι ὁ Ραμαζὰν πῶς κοίταζε κατάματα τὸ θάνατο,
μέρες ὁλόκληρες μέσα στὸ χιόνι τῆς Ἀνατολῆς
στὸν παγωμένον ἥλιο
κατάματα μέρες ὁλόκληρες ὁ μικρὸς ἐφέστιος θεός.
Μὴ σταθεῖς ταξιδιώτη.
«Τρία καρτίνια ἀριστερὰ» μουρμούρισε ὁ τιμονιέρης.

...ἴσως ὁ φίλος μου νὰ κοντοστέκουνταν,
ξέμπαρκος τώρα
κλειστὸς σ' ἕνα μικρὸ σπίτι μὲ εἰκόνες
γυρεύοντας παράθυρα πίσω ἀπ' τὰ κάδρα.
Χτύπησε ἡ καμπάνα τοῦ καραβιοῦ
σὰν τὴ μονέδα πολιτείας ποὺ χάθηκε
κι ἦρθε νὰ ζωντανέψει πέφτοντας
ἀλλοτινὲς ἐλεημοσύνες.

The Cats of St. Nicholas

> *Yet still the emotional instinct,*
> *self-taught from within,*
> *intones a dirge of the Avenging Spirit*
> *without a lyre,*
> *without having at all*
> *the beloved audacity of hope.*
> *—Aeschylus's Agamemnon*

"The Feline Cape is now visible," said my friend the captain
while pointing out a low beach in the fog.
The shore was empty on Christmas Day,
"and far off to the West is where the wave gave birth to Aphrodite.
They call the place Greek Rock.
Three quarter-winds to the left!"
In another time I lost a cat who had the eyes of Salome
and then one named Ramazan who held death's gaze
for days on end in the snow of Anatolia
and in the frozen sun,
right in the eyes for days on end, that little household god.
Don't pause, traveler.
"Three quarter-winds to the left," murmured the helmsman.

Perhaps my friend is retired now,
no longer at sea,
shut up in a small house with icons and
seeking the windows behind iron grilles.
The ship's bell rang—
a piece of our commonwealth that was lost
but revived when it found
compassion from a bygone era.

«Παράξενο», ξανάειπε ὁ καπετάνιος.
«Τούτη ἡ καμπάνα —μέρα ποὺ εἶναι—
μοῦ θύμισε τὴν ἄλλη ἐκείνη, τὴ μοναστηρίσια.
Διηγότανε τὴν ἱστορία ἕνας καλόγερος
ἕνας μισότρελος, ἕνας ὀνειροπόλος.

»Τὸν καιρὸ τῆς μεγάλης στέγνιας,
—σαράντα χρόνια ἀναβροχιὰ—
ρημάχτηκε ὅλο τὸ νησί
πέθαινε ὁ κόσμος καὶ γεννιοῦνταν φίδια.
Μιλιούνια φίδια τοῦτο τ' ἀκρωτήρι,
χοντρὰ σὰν τὸ ποδάρι ἀνθρώπου
καὶ φαρμακερά.
Τὸ μοναστήρι τ' Ἀι-Νικόλα τὸ εἶχαν τότε
Ἀγιοβασιλεῖτες καλογέροι
κι οὔτε μποροῦσαν νὰ δουλέψουν τὰ χωράφια
κι οὔτε νὰ βγάλουν τὰ κοπάδια στὴ βοσκή·
τοὺς ἔσωσαν οἱ γάτες ποὺ ἀναθρέφαν.
Τὴν κάθε αὐγὴ χτυποῦσε μιὰ καμπάνα
καὶ ξεκινοῦσαν τσοῦρμο γιὰ τὴ μάχη.
Ὅλη μέρα χτυπιοῦνταν ὡς τὴν ὥρα
ποὺ σήμαιναν τὸ βραδινὸ ταγίνι.
Ἀπόδειπνα πάλι ἡ καμπάνα
καὶ βγαῖναν γιὰ τὸν πόλεμο τῆς νύχτας.
Ἤτανε θαῦμα νὰ τὶς βλέπεις, λένε,
ἄλλη κουτσή, κι ἄλλη στραβή, τὴν ἄλλη
χωρὶς μύτη, χωρὶς αὐτί, προβιὰ κουρέλι.
Ἔτσι μὲ τέσσερεις καμπάνες τὴν ἡμέρα
πέρασαν μῆνες, χρόνια, καιροὶ κι ἄλλοι καιροί.
Ἄγρια πεισματικὲς καὶ πάντα λαβωμένες
ξολόθρεψαν τὰ φίδια μὰ στὸ τέλος
χαθήκανε· δὲν ἄντεξαν τόσο φαρμάκι.

The captain broke the silence. "It's strange,
this bell—on this day—
reminds me of that other bell, the one at the monastery."
He told the story of a monk,
half-crazed, driven by dreams.

"During the time of the great drought—
forty years it lasted—
the whole island was ruined.
Lots of people died and snakes proliferated.
Millions of snakes filled that cape,
each one thick like a foot
and poisonous.
At that time the monastery of St. Nicholas
was held by the monks of St. Basil
and they couldn't work the fields
or graze herds.
The cats they fed saved them.
Each morning a bell rang
and the crew left for battle.
All day they pounded on each other until
the signal for the evening meal.
After dinner the bell rang again
and they went out for the night's warfare.
They say it was a miracle to behold—
one was limping, another bowlegged, others
missing a nose, an ear, fur shredded.
And so with four bells a day, months went by,
years, ages, and more ages.
Ferally stubborn and constantly wounded,
they exterminated the snakes.
But in the end they died too—
they couldn't handle so much poison.

Ὡσὰν καράβι καταποντισμένο
τίποτε δὲν ἀφῆσαν στὸν ἀφρὸ
μήτε νιαούρισμα, μήτε καμπάνα.
Γραμμή!
Τί νὰ σοῦ κάνουν οἱ ταλαίπωρες
παλεύοντας καὶ πίνοντας μέρα καὶ νύχτα
τὸ αἷμα τὸ φαρμακερὸ τῶν ἑρπετῶν.
Αἰῶνες φαρμάκι· γενιὲς φαρμάκι».
«Γραμμή!» ἀντιλάλησε ἀδιάφορος ὁ τιμονιέρης.

Τετάρτη, 5 Φεβρουαρίου 1969

Like a sunken ship,
nothing was left behind in the foam,
not a meow, not a bell.
Line!
        What more could they do, the poor things,
battling and imbibing the venomous
blood, day and night.
Eons of poison. Generations of poison."
"Line!" echoed the helmsman in indifference.

Wednesday, February 5, 1969

Ὀλυμπία, Κ΄ αἰ. μ.Χ.

Τοῦ Γιώργη Παυλόπουλου

Ἡ Δεσποινὶς Πίτυς ἐδῶ λατρεύει τοὺς ἀρχαίους.
Στενάζει μὲ τὸ βιαστικὸ Βοριὰ
μὲ τὸ Νοτιὰ δακρύζει·
πιάνει βελόνες καὶ κεντᾶ
κεντᾶ κεντᾶ
μὲ τὸ Γαρμπὴ καὶ τὸ Σιρόκο.

Ἡ Δεσποινὶς Πίτυς ὀνειρεύτηκε τὴν αὐγὴ
πὼς τὴν κοιμοῦνταν ἕνας Λάπιθος κι ἀφοῦ τὴ χάρηκε
ξανάγινε ἄγαλμα σὲ κάποια στέγη·
τὸν ἔχει ἀκόμη στὴν ψυχή της, τέτοιο ἀγόρι.

Καθὼς ἀνέβαινε σήμερα στὴν ἐκκλησιὰ
ψηλὰ στὸ Δρούβα μὲ μαύρη μούλα
αὐτὸν συλλογίζουνταν.
Μέρα τ' Ἁι-Γιώργη καὶ τὸ εἰκόνισμα ζωσμένο
γλυσίνες ἢ πασχαλιές, καθὼς τὶς λὲν οἱ ντόπιοι·
λειτουργάει ὁ Παπακένταυρος.

Ἡ Δεσποινὶς Πίτυς προσεύχεται, μιὰ κίνηση στὰ χείλια της
    τὸ δείχνει
ἢ μήπως εἶναι σχῆμα τοῦ φιλιοῦ;
Πίσω της ἀθέατος, λαίμαργος κι ἀπίστευτα παρὼν
ὁ ΠΙΤΥΟΚΑΜΠΤΗΣ

1963 – Μάης 1970

Olympia, Twentieth Century AD

for George Pavlopoulos

Here Miss Pine worships the ancients.
She sighs with the quick north wind
and weeps with the south wind.
She takes up needles and sews—
stitch stitch—
with the southwesterly and southeasterly winds.

Miss Pine dreams of the dawn
when a Lapith took her to bed and after enjoying her
returned to being a statue on some roof.
She can still feel him in her soul, this young man.

As she climbed the hill to church today,
up to Drouva with a black mule,
she was thinking of him.
It's the feast day of St. George and
the icon stand is woven with wisteria,
though the locals call them lilies.
The Centaur Priest officiates the liturgy.

Miss Pine is saying her prayers,
you can tell by the motion of her lips—
or are they making the shape of a kiss?
Behind her, unseen yet present,
incredibly insatiable—
stands the *Pine Bender*.

1963–May 1970

Ἵππιος Κολωνὸς

Τ' ἀηδόνια καὶ τὰ λιόδεντρα
τὰ σάρωσαν οἱ πολυκατοικίες
οἱ ἄνθρωποι σκόρπισαν ἐμπρὸς στὶς μηχανές.

Στὴν κορυφὴ τοῦ λόφου ἕνα πουλάρι
κοίταζε ἀγέρωχα ὥρα τὴν Ἀθήνα
χλιμίντρισε ξαναχλιμίντρισε
καὶ τ' ἄκουσα νὰ λέει «Γιαχοὺ»
στυλώνοντας τ' αὐτιά του.
Ἔπειτα ἐλεύθερο μ' ὀλόρθη οὐρὰ
γλάκησε κατὰ τὴν κατηφόρα.

Μάης 1970

Horsey Hill in Kolonos

The nightingales and olive trees
were swept away by the high-rises;
people scattered before the machines.

A foal on the hill's summit
glared long and hard at Athens
with a smart-ass look.
He neighed and whinnied,
pricking up his ears,
                    and I heard him say "Yahoo!"
Willfully then,
with his tail straight up,
he hurtled down the hill.

May 1970

«Ἐπὶ ἀσπαλάθων...»

Ἦταν ὡραῖο τὸ Σούνιο τὴ μέρα ἐκείνη τοῦ Εὐαγγελισμοῦ
πάλι μὲ τὴν ἄνοιξη.
Λιγοστὰ πράσινα φύλλα γύρω στὶς σκουριασμένες πέτρες
τὸ κόκκινο χῶμα κι ἀσπάλαθοι
δείχνοντας ἕτοιμα τὰ μεγάλα τους βελόνια
καὶ τοὺς κίτρινους ἀνθούς.
Ἀπόμακρα οἱ ἀρχαῖες κολόνες, χορδὲς μιᾶς ἅρπας ἀντηχοῦν
ἀκόμη...

Γαλήνη.
— Τί μπορεῖ νὰ μοῦ θύμισε τὸν Ἀρδιαῖο ἐκεῖνον;
Μιὰ λέξη στὸν Πλάτωνα θαρρῶ, χαμένη στοῦ μυαλοῦ
τ' αὐλάκια·
τ' ὄνομα τοῦ κίτρινου θάμνου
δὲν ἄλλαξε ἀπὸ ἐκείνους τοὺς καιρούς.
Τὸ βράδυ βρῆκα τὴν περικοπή:
«Τὸν ἔδεσαν χειροπόδαρα» μᾶς λέει
«τὸν ἔριξαν χάμω καὶ τὸν ἔγδαραν
τὸν ἔσυραν παράμερα τὸν καταξέσκισαν
ἀπάνω στοὺς ἀγκαθεροὺς ἀσπάλαθους
καὶ πῆγαν καὶ τὸν πέταξαν στὸν Τάρταρο, κουρέλι».

Ἔτσι στὸν κάτω κόσμο πλέρωνε τὰ κρίματά του
ὁ Παμφύλιος Ἀρδιαῖος ὁ πανάθλιος Τύραννος.

31 τοῦ Μάρτη 1971

"On the Aspalathus..."

Spring returned
and on that day of the Annunciation
ancient Sounion was beautiful:
a few green leaves around rust-colored stones,
the red earth, and gorse bushes
displaying their huge thorns at the ready,
with yellow flowers, too.
In the distance stood the ancient columns,
while strains of plunder still echoed in the air—

Serenity.
What could have reminded me of that Ardiaeus?
I believe it was only one word in Plato's *Republic*, lost in the
  recesses of my mind.
The name for that yellow bush
hasn't changed since then.
That evening I found the passage:
"They bound him hand and foot," it tells us,
"they cast him down and flayed him,
dragged him aside and tore him to shreds
on the thorny aspalathus.
Then they hurled him into Tartarus, tattered."

That's how he paid for his crimes in the underworld,
Ardiaeus of Pamphylia, the most wretched tyrant.

March 31, 1971

Περιστατικὰ (1931-1971)

Circumstantial Poems (1931–1971)

Ἰνδικὸ παραμύθι

Κάτω ἀπ᾽ τὶς κουβαροσουκιὲς
κάθεται ἡ λωτομάτα
κόβει ντομάτα γιὰ σαλάτα
καδάμπες καὶ γαντζιές.

Πῶς τραγουδεῖ τζιντζιριστὰ
κι οἱ μπαμπουκαλαμιῶνες
μὲ τοὺς ἀμπανοζιοδεντρῶνες
γνέφουνται στὰ λιμνιά...

Ὤ, φρίκη! ξάφνου ἀπ᾽ τοὺς δρυμοὺς
πηδήσανε οἱ ἀρτζοῦνες!
Μὲ κάτι φλογερὲς μουτσοῦνες
καὶ μὲ κακοὺς σκοποὺς

κινήσανε κοπαδιαστὰ
νὰ βροῦν τὸν ἄσο κούπα
τῆς κόρης ποὺ ἦταν σὰν τουλούπα
στοῦ Γάγγη τὰ νερά...

Μὰ ἡ διαλεχτὴ τῶν Νισχιαντχῶν
ἀρτζοῦνες δὲν ἐσκιάχτη
καὶ στὸ κοπάδι ἔβγαλε τ᾽ ἄχτι
τ᾽ ἀψὺ τῶν Βινταρμπχῶν.

Κι ὅταν ἐφύγαν μουλωχτὰ
πέρα στὶς ἀμαλάκες
εἶπε: «Ἄ᾽ στὸ διάολο μαλάκες!...»
κι ἔφαγε ἀνόρεχτα.

Λονδίνο, 7.11.1931

Indian Folktale

Underneath the tangled fig trees
sat a man with lotus eyes,
slicing salad tomatoes,
sandalwood, and acacia tree flowers.

Oh song of the ginger man!
He sang, as bamboo slingers
nodded to ebony sawyers
circling the lagoons...

Oh the terror! Suddenly
Arjunas leapt from the trees
with flaming sneers
and evil schemes!

Driving everyone into a herd
to find the crown jewel of the Nishad
delicate as a muslin gown
in the waters of the Ganges...

Yet the chosen maiden of the Nishad
Arjunas didn't blanch
and in the herd a grudge
aroused the Vidarbhans.
When they had skulked away,

the lotus-eyed man,
sitting among the amalaki trees,
said, "Those assholes can go to hell!"
and ate dejectedly.

London, November 7, 1931

Μπαλάδα

Στὸν Γιῶργο Κατσίμπαλη

Ἐσώσαμε στὴ ζήση μιὰν αὐγὴ
πού 'λαμπε σὰ χρουσάργυρο μαγνάδι·
ἡ ψή μας 'τρόμασσε ἀπὸ τὴ γοργὴ
λαχτάρα μας, ἀρίφνητο κοπάδι.
Δὲν ξεύροντας τὰ μάτια μας ὁμάδι
νὰ μάθουσι γυρεύγασι μακριὰ
στὸ πέλαγο, στὸ δάσο, τὴ βαθιὰ
βουλὴ ποὺ μᾶς ἐχάρισε ἔτοια μέρα
κι ἀγάλι-ἀγάλι τό 'σαζε ἡ φιλιὰ
νὰ χτίζομε περβόλια στὸν ἀγέρα.

Πῶς τὸ δεντρὸ ἀψηλώνει τὴν κορφὴ
τὴν ἄνοιξη κι εἶν' στὰ πουλιὰ σημάδι
ἡ πείραξη τοῦ νοῦ, προθυμερή,
πεντάπλουμη, μὲ δίχως ἀσκημάδι,
μᾶς κόμπωνε μὲς στὸ κουρφὸ λαγκάδι
τοῦ κόσμου ποὺ δὲν ἔχει γνωριμιά.
Χαρακωμένοι στὴν ἀνημποριὰ
μπλιὸ δὲ λογιάζαμε νιότη οὐδὲ γέρα
πασκίζοντας νὰ βροῦμε μιὰ φωλιὰ
νὰ χτίζομε περβόλια στὸν ἀγέρα.

Ἄθος ἡ ἀθιβολὴ ἡ ἀλλοτινὴ
κι ἡ σιγανάδα ποὺ ἅπλωνε ὡσὰν λάδι·
δὲν εἶναι ταχινὴ οὐδὲ ἀργατινὴ
τὸ κάρβουνό μας βράζει στὸ σκοτάδι.
Ἡ πρίκα μας σκληρὸ προσκεφαλάδι
κι ἡ λησμονιὰ ξαγριεύει τὴν ξενιά,
κι ἡ θύμηση γιαγέρνει μ' ἀπονιά,
νὰ λέει τὴν κρίση ὅπου τὰ πάθη φέρα,

Ballad

for George Katsimbalis

At daybreak, our lives were redeemed.
Dawn gleamed like a gilded veil.
Our souls recoiled at the charge
of our desires, infinitely teeming.
Seeking knowledge, our eyes roamed:
sea, forest, and the depths of our intention,
by the day bestowed. Drop by drop
we imbibed it in our camaraderie:
the will to build a heavenly paradise.

Like the way a tree in bloom lifts the skyline
and is an omen for the birds, our mental exercise,
in its fivefold avidity, was a thing of beauty.
But it tricked us into the world's yawning chasm,
ignorant. Scored by ineptitude's toil, neither
youth nor senility had any significance
while we strove to find a nest
to build our heavenly gardens.
Our conversations became yesterday's

ashes, with a quiet that spread like oil.
Deprived of the morning light,
our coal burned through the night.
A heavy grief weighed on our brows.
Diversion inflamed withdrawal,
remembrance restored apathy,
in crisis, our desires longed
to speak their woe.

κι ἀπόμεινέ μας μοναχὴ γιατρειὰ
νὰ χτίζομε περβόλια στὸν ἀγέρα

Στάλσιμο

Μοίρα ποὺ μᾶς ἐπῆρες τὴν ἐξιά,
μὴ γδικιωθεῖς, τ' ἀκάτεχα κορμιὰ
τὸ δὲν τὰ μαστορέψα δὲν τὸ ξέρα,
βούηθα κι ἀλάφρωνέ μας τὴν καρδιὰ
νὰ χτίζομε περβόλια στὸν ἀγέρα.

Λονδίνο, 10.11.1931

Only one remedy remained:
to build a heavenly paradise.

* * Petition * *

Fate who stole our power,
hold back your vengeance.
I didn't know how to fix
untrained bodies.
Help us, lighten our hearts,
so that we can build a heavenly paradise.

London, November 10, 1931

Καὶ τοῦτο τοῦ Σεφέρη. Στὸ Φαβρίκιο
ποὺ μὲς στὸ βρίκιο
«Ἀργώ», ἐνῶ ἡ ἑταίρα
σηκώνει τὰ μεριά της στὸν ἀγέρα
καὶ τὸν κυκλώνουν ἀφροδίσιοι ἴσκιοι,
κοιτάζει ἀλάργα καὶ τραβάει οὐίσκι.

Λονδίνο, [4.11.1933]

This round's on Seferis.
For Fabrice, who's on the brig
Argo, while the call girl
lifts her cheeks for a whirl,
and he, surrounded by ghosts feeling frisky,
looks off in the distance and sips his whiskey.

London, November 4, 1933

Ἀπάνω στ' ἅρματα μεγάλες στολὲς καὶ λοφία
ἔπειτα:
            Οἱ μανάδες καὶ τὰ παιδιὰ
θὰ προχωροῦν εὐλαβικὰ μὲ σκυμμένο τὸ κεφάλι
χωρὶς φωνὲς καὶ χωρὶς κλάματα
(κοσμιότης προπάντων στὰ φορέματα τῶν κυριῶν καὶ στὰ
    ψιμμύθια)
θ' ἀκολουθοῦν οἱ πρεσβύτεροι μὲ τὴ μεγαλοπρέπεια
ποὺ τοὺς ἐπιβάλλουν οἱ νόμοι τῆς πολιτείας·
τέλος οἱ ἔφηβοι μαζὶ μὲ τὶς ὥριμες κόρες
(ἀμφίεσις γυμναστηρίου· ἀπαγορεύονται οἱ στηθόδεσμοι κι οἱ
    ἄσεμνες χειρονομίες).
Συγκέντρωση μπροστὰ στὸ Ζάππειο ὥρα 8 μ.μ.
Ἡ Συνοδεία θὰ ξεκινήσει μὲ τάξη ἀκολουθώντας
τὴ λεωφόρο Ἀμαλίας καὶ τὴν ὁδὸ
Διονυσίου τοῦ Ἀρεοπαγίτου
ὣς τὰ προπύλαια τῆς Ἀκρόπολης. Οἱ λαμπαδηφόροι
θὰ δίνουν κάθε ἑκατὸ βήματα τὸ σημάδι
τῆς ἐξιλαστήριας κραυγῆς.
Ἡ ἀστυνομία θὰ φροντίσει ν' ἀπαγορέψει
τὴν κυκλοφορία τῶν τροχοφόρων τὰ κάστανα
τὸ πασατέμπο καὶ τὰ μεγάφωνα.
Οἱ Σεμνὲς ὑποσχέθηκαν στὸν ἐπίσκοπο-Ἀρχιερέα
νὰ ξαναμποῦνε στὸ σπήλαιό τους
καὶ μένοντας ἐκεῖ νὰ προστατεύουν τὴν πόλη
ὣς τὴ συντέλεια τῶν αἰώνων. Τὸ πρόσταξε ὁ Θεὸς τῆς
    Ἑλλάδος.
Ὀλολύξατε νῦν ἐπὶ μολπαῖς
νῦν ἐπὶ μολπαῖς
ὀλολύξατε...

Ὀκτώβρης 1934

At the head, soldiers at arms in uniform and crests.
Next:
        Mothers and children
will proceed with piety, heads bowed,
without shouting and tears.
(Above all, women should be decorous in dresses and
    makeup.)
Elders will follow with the grandeur
prescribed by our laws.
Lastly, young men and women dressed in exercise attire.
(Brassieres and disrespectful gestures are prohibited.)
Meeting point in front of the Zappeion at 8 p.m.
The procession will leave in order
following Amalias Avenue and Dionysius the Areopagite Street
until the gates of the Acropolis.
The torchbearers will give the sign for the propitiatory cry
every hundred steps.
The police will make sure to prevent
the circulation of vehicles, chestnuts,
pumpkin seeds, and megaphones.
The Respectful Furies promised the Bishop-High Priest
to return to their cave
and, remaining there, to protect the city
until the end of time. The God of Greece ordered it.
Cry out now, in joyful song and dance!
Now in joyful song and dance!
Cry out!

October 1934

Ὁ τελευταῖος χορὸς

Ἕνα παραλλαγμένο παραμύθι ξεπληρώνουμε κι ἐμεῖς
καὶ οἱ ἄλλοι
ὅπως κι οἱ ἀποτεφρωμένοι γέροντες
ποὺ εἶχαν ραβδιὰ στὰ χέρια καὶ μιλοῦσαν ἤρεμα.
Τὸ βουρκωμένο λουτρό, τὸ δίχτυ, τὸ μαχαίρι
ἡ πορφύρα κι ἡ φωνὴ ποὺ ρωτοῦσε γιὰ τὴ θάλασσα
ποιὸς θὰ τὴν ἐξαντλήσει,
θρέψανε τὴ ζωή μας.
Τὴν ἀγάπη μας τὴν πίναμε σιγὰ-σιγὰ
μᾶς φαίνουνταν καταπότιο γιὰ μιθριδατισμό·
ὥσπου τὸ τέλος ἦρθε κι ἀπονεκρώθηκε.
Ἀλήθεια, πάντα φρόνιμα μᾶς ὁδήγησε
ὁ λαός μας.

Ἀρκείτω βίος, τούτη ἡ ζωὴ
ἀνάμεσα Πεντέλη καὶ Ὑμηττὸ καὶ Πάρνηθα.
Ὅμως οἱ ρίζες
οἱ ρίζες δὲ μαραίνουνται εὔκολα
δὲ φεύγουν εὔκολα τὰ μιάσματα
τῆς ἀλλοφροσύνης, τῆς ἀδικίας, τῆς κενοσπουδίας.
Τρεῖς χιλιάδες χρόνια καὶ περισσότερα
πάνω στοὺς ἴδιους βράχους
πληρώνουμε τὸ παραλλαγμένο παραμύθι.
Λυπήσου ἐκείνους ποὺ περιμένουν!

26.11.1934

The Final Chorus

An altered folktale—that's what we're paying off.
All the others too—
like our elders who held canes and spoke serenely
and were reduced to ashes.
The murky bath, the net, the knife,
the deep-hued purple and the voice that questioned the sea—
who could drain it—
these symbols nourished our life.
We imbibed our love drop by drop.
It seemed a poison pill to build our immunity—
until the end came and our love was eradicated.
Truly, our people always guided us
with prudence.

Enough of life, this life
encircled by Mounts Pendeli and Hymettus and Parnitha.
But the roots—
the roots don't wither easily.
They don't easily disappear—
the defilements
of madness, of injustice, of vain pursuits.
We're paying off an altered folktale
on these very same rocks
for three thousand years and more.
Pity those who are yet to come!

November 26, 1934

Ένας στοιχειοθέτης παρεφρόνησε
(Ταγκὸ)

Στοιχεῖα τῶν ἔξι, κι ἂν πηγαίνουν
στὸ Λουτράκι, στὸ Πήλιο, στὰ Καμένα Βοῦρλα
κι ἂν πηγαίνουν στ' ἄσπρα νησιὰ ποὺ ἀνάβουνε στὸν ἥλιο
στὸν ἥμερο γιαλὸ μὲ τὰ κορίτσια, κι ἂν πηγαίνουν
τὰ μικρὰ στοιχεῖα τῶν ἔξι στιγμῶν κάθε στιγμή,
κι ἃ φεύγουν μέσα στὸν ἥλιο
ποὺ κάνει τὸ δέρμα πετιμέζι μὲ τὸ τραγούδι τοῦ φωνογράφου,
τὰ μικρὰ νούμερα τῶν ἔξι στιγμῶν, ἐμεῖς
μαζεύουμε γράμμα τὸ γράμμα κάθε λέξη
πολεμώντας νὰ κολλήσουμε τὸ ἕνα μὲ τ' ἄλλο, ἐμεῖς
τὰ μικρὰ νούμερα.

Κι ἂν πηγαίνουν διαβάζοντας ἐφημερίδες
κι ἂν κάθουνται σ' ἐφτὰ καρέκλες
μὲ τὸ γυμνὸ κορίτσι στὴν τρίτη σελίδα,
τ' ἄρωμά της,
σὰν ἔσκυψε νὰ διορθώσει τὰ δοκίμια —
«νὰ τὸ χαρεῖς ἄφησα τὸ κορμί μου»
κι εἶδα τὰ μῆλα τυπωμένα μὲ στοιχεῖα τῶν ἔξι
μὲ κεφαλαῖα κόκκινα, καὶ τρέμαν
«γιὰ νὰ περάσουν μόνο τὴ βραδιά τους» — κι ἂν πηγαίνουν
μὲ τὶς ποιήτριες στὸ πιεστήριο τὰ κόκκινα μῆλα,
τὰ μικρὰ νούμερα πηγαίνουν.

7.7.1935

A Stanza Composer Cracks Up

(Tango)

A composition in hexasyllables,
does it fly in Loutraki,
does it fly in Pelion,
or Kamena Vourla?
Does it fly on islands of white
that ascend into the sun
with girls on docile beaches?
Do short lines of six beats
ever align, or do they flee
into the sunlight
that sweetens your skin like syrup,
while a phonograph croons?
Short numbers of six beats, we
arrange each word letter by letter,
struggling to stick them together,
we of the short numbers.

Do they land while reading newspapers
and do they sit in seven seats
with a naked girl on page three?
Oh her perfume,
as she leans over, correcting the features—
"I left my body here for your pleasure,"
she wrote, and I saw her
breasts with red capitals,
apples printed in hexasyllables,
vibrating, "just for one night only."
And if they make it with poetesses
at the press's red apples,
then short numbers really do fly.

July 7, 1935

Ὁ κ. Φιλοποίμην Α. Παχυμέρης χορεύει

Νόθος πατέρας τοῦ Ι. Κωλέττη ἢ ἀντίδικος τοῦ Διονυσίου κόμητος Σολωμοῦ,
χορεύει στὸ φῶς τῆς ἀσετιλίνης ποὺ ἀψηλώνει τ' ἄστρα τοῦ βουνοῦ,
χορεύει ἀνάμεσα στὶς Αἰγυπτιώτισσες προικοφόρες καὶ στοὺς πρωινοὺς ἀγωγιάτες,
ἐνῶ τὸ δεξὶ παράλυτο χέρι του τρέμει ἑτοιμοθάνατο πάνω σὲ εἰκοσάχρονες πλάτες.
Ἔξω ἀπὸ τὸν κύκλο τοῦ φωτὸς ἡ νύχτα γεμάτη καστανιὲς καὶ τριζόνια
σκύβει καὶ χύνεται στὸ πέλαγο ποὺ περιμένει νὰ ἐξαντληθοῦν τὰ χρόνια·
νὰ τελειώσουν οἱ συζητήσεις μας γιὰ τὴ βασιλεία καὶ τὴ δημοκρατία,
ἡ κομματιασμένη μας ζωὴ σὲ καρέκλες καὶ σὲ τραπεζάκια, μὲ τόσην ἀπιστία.
Ὅμως ὁ κ. Παχυμέρης, Φιλοποίμην τοῦ Ἀμβροσίου,
χορεύει ἕνα μελίπηκτο ταγκό, ὀγδοντάρης συνταξιοῦχος τοῦ λαθρεμπορίου.
Ἔμπορος φτερῶν στρουθοκαμήλου, χρηματοδότης τοῦ Ἀλ Καπόνε, τ' ἀνίψια του (τριάντα) περιμένουν
νὰ πεθάνει.
Ὅμως τὴν ὕστατη στιγμή, τὴν ὥριμη χολή, ποιὸς δὲ γυρεύει νὰ τὴ γλυκάνει,
κι ἂς παίζει αὐτὸς ὁ μαῦρος ἄνθρωπος, ἄλλοτε τρόφιμος κάποιου φρενοκομείου τῆς Κερκύρας,
ἕνα βιολὶ ναυαγισμένο στὰ χέρια του ποὺ ὑποδύεται τὴν ἀδικία τῆς μοίρας,
χορεύει ὁ κ. Παχυμέρης· ἡ κόρη ποὺ ἀγκαλιάζει εἶναι ὄμορφη· μόλις βγῆκε ἀπὸ τὸ ΓΑΛΛΙΚΟ παρθεναγωγεῖο·
τῆς ἔταξε, ἂν χορέψει μαζί του καὶ στὰ σκοτεινά, νὰ δώσει λεφτὰ γιὰ τὸ κοινοτικὸ ὑδραγωγεῖο.

Mr. Lovemaker A. Fatass Dances

He's dancing in the acetylene light that elevates stars on the
mountaintop,
the bastard father of Ioannis Kolettis, or adversary of Dionysius,
Earl of Solomos.
He dances between Egyptian girls bearing dowries and
between morning cart drivers,
while his crippled right hand trembles on the verge of death,
dangling above the backs of twenty-year-olds.
Beyond the circle of light, the night is full of chestnut trees and
insects.
He bends down and immerses himself into the sea and the sea
waits for time to be exhausted,
for the end of our discussions about the king and democracy,
the end of our fragmented life in chairs and at café tables, our
life so lacking in faith.
Still, Mr. Fatass, Ambrosial Lovemaker,
dances a saccharine tango, this 80-year-old retiree of the
black market.
Merchant of ostrich plumes, financial backer of Al Capone, his
nieces and nephews (30 of them) wait for him to die.
Yet in the height of the moment, in the height of ire, who
wouldn't want to make it sweeter?
Why not let this dark man play—a busted violin in his hands
mimicking the injustice of fate—
he who was once a patient at some asylum in Corfu.
Mr. Fatass dances. The girl in his embrace is beautiful; she's
just left a French girls' school.
He promised her, if she danced with him in the darkness, that
he would donate to the public waterworks.

Ὁ κ. Παχυμέρης, Φαβρίκιε, εἶναι ἄνθρωπος τῆς
πραγματικότητας καὶ ξέρει νὰ τὴν ἀντιμετωπίσει.
Λέει πὼς ἡ ψυχὴ εἶναι «ἀσθένεια ποὺ κάποτε ὁ πολιτισμὸς θὰ
τὴν ἐξοβελίσει».
Λατρεύει τὴν «ἐπιστήμη» καὶ τὸ κονφόρ· μισεῖ τὴν τέχνη· θά
'δινε 100.000 ντάλλαρς γιὰ νὰ μὴν ὑπάρχει.
Σὲ τοῦτο βρίσκει σύμφωνο καὶ τὸν τοπικὸ κομματάρχη
ποὺ κάθε βράδυ συζητᾶ μὲ τὸν καθαρευουσιάνο δάσκαλο
περὶ τοῦ ἀρχαίου ἑλληνικοῦ κλέους
καὶ περὶ τῶν δοξασιῶν τῆς Δύσεως ποὺ διαφθείρουν τοὺς
νέους...
Μέσα στὸ σκοτάδι οἱ καστανιές, τὸ πέλαγο, οἱ Σποράδες καὶ
τὰ τριζόνια
προσμένουν, ἔξω ἀπ' τὴν πραγματικότητα νὰ περάσουν τὰ
χρόνια. Θεοί, πόσα χρόνια;

Ζαγορά, 6.8.1935

Mr. Fatass, you see Fabrice, is a man of reality and he knows
how to confront it.
He says that the soul is "a sickness that civilization will
eliminate eventually."
He worships "science" and comfort. He hates art; he would
give 100,000 dollars if it would mean that art ceased to
exist.
In this he agrees with the local political boss
who each night meets with his teacher to discuss ancient
Hellenic glory in purified Greek
and the doctrines of the West that corrupt young people.

Deep in the darkness the chestnut trees, the sea, the Sporades
islands, and the insects wait,
beyond reality, for time to pass.
Gods, how many years?

Zagora, August 6, 1935

Λεωφόρος Συγγρού, Β΄

Ἡ λεωφόρο Συγγροῦ, τὸ γιοφύρι μὲ τοὺς δυὸ κόλπους καὶ τὶς δυὸ
κορυφές,
ποὺ μᾶς δοκίμαζε καὶ τὴ δοκιμάζαμε, ἀφήνοντας τὶς προσεχτικὲς
γραφές,
ὥσπου νὰ βροῦμε τὴ θάλασσα γεμάτη πίκρα καὶ στοργή, γαλήνια,
γαλάζια,
γραμμένη μέσα σὲ νησιά, στολισμένη μὲ βαπόρια καὶ καράβια·
ἡ λεωφόρο Συγγροῦ πλατιὰ καὶ μυστικὴ κρύβοντας κι ἀργοπορώντας
κι ἔπειτα δείχνοντας ξαφνικὰ
τὸ κορμὶ τῆς γοργόνας γυμνό, μὲ ξέπλεκα ὡς τὸν ὁρίζοντα μαλλιά,
μὲ δέρμα τριανταφυλλί, βυθισμένο λιγάκι στὸ κρασάτο νερό, μὲ τὸ
στῆθος
ἀναγυρτὸ καὶ κόκκινο στὴν ἄκρη καθὼς ἔπαιρνε νὰ βασιλέψει ὁ ἥλιος·
ὁ δρόμος μὲ τὶς φρόνιμες πιπεριές, ἀλλὰ ὁ δρόμος ποὺ μᾶς ἔμαθε
τὴ γυμναστικὴ
ν' ἀφήνεις κάποτε τοὺς φίλους, τὴν ἀγάπη καὶ τὴ μουσικὴ
γιὰ νὰ ξεκινήσεις χωρὶς νὰ ξέρεις ποῦ θὰ σὲ βγάλει ἡ ἄκρη —
Εἶδε ἕνα ὄνειρο, Φαβρίκιε, βυθισμένος σὲ μιὰ λουλακιὰ ποὺ τὸν
ἔπνιγε νάρκη:
Δὲν ἦταν ὁ Μουσολίνι ποὺ ἔκανε πόλεμο τοῦ Ράς, ἤμαστε ἐμεῖς,
ἤμαστε ἐμεῖς οἱ Ρωμιοί· καὶ μᾶς πῆραν οἱ Αἰθίοπες τὸ κατόπι
καὶ ρίξαν καράβια στὸ γιαλό, καὶ στεῖλαν κήρυκες, κι εἶπαν: «Ἄνθρωποι,
σεῖς ποὺ μαλώνετε καὶ σαλιαρίζετε, ποὺ τὰ πάντα ἀρχίζετε καὶ
δὲν τελειώνετε καμιὰ πράξη,
ἀποφασίσαμε —μιὰ ποὺ τὶς φάγατε— νὰ σᾶς δώσουμε ἕνα βασιλιὰ
νὰ σᾶς βάλει σὲ τάξη».
Κι ἐμεῖς —μιὰ ποὺ τὶς φάγαμε— γιὰ νὰ εἴμαστε συνεπεῖς, κράξαμε
ἀμέσως «Ζήτω ἡ βασιλεία!»
κάναμε κι ἕνα δημοψήφισμα, γιὰ νὰ φανεῖ πὼς εἴμαστε λαὸς μ'
ἐλευθερία.
Κι ἔφτασε ὁ βασιλιὰς στὶς Τζιτζιφιές, μὲ φτερὰ καὶ μὲ γένια σγουρά,
πολὺ μελαψός, ὁ Ρὰς Πουπουναμπί.

Syngrou Avenue II

Syngrou Avenue, the bridge with two gulfs and two hills,
this road tested us and we tested it, leaving aside our
careful writings,
until we found the sea, full of sorrow and affection, calm,
cerulean,
channeled between islands, adorned with ferries and boats.
Syngrou Avenue, broad and enigmatic, concealing and
delaying and then suddenly revealing
the body of the naked mermaid, her hair unraveled,
spreading on the horizon,
with rosy skin, half-submerged in the wine-dark water,
with her spherical breasts,
outlined in red as the sun started to set.
The road with the prudent pepper trees, but also the one
that taught us how to exercise,
sometimes how to let go of friends, love, and music,
how to set out without knowing when you'll reach your limit—
You see, Fabrice, the road dreamt, submerged in an indigo stupor:
It wasn't Mussolini who waged war on Ras Tafari, it was us.
We were the *Romioi*; and Ethiopia pursued us by sea,
they sent boats and messengers who said, "People,
you who quarrel and blather, who start everything and never
finish anything,
we've decided—now that you've bit the dust—to give you
a king and put you in your place."
And we, to be polite—since we bit the dust—shouted
automatically, "Long live the king!"
We had a referendum so that we would seem to be a people
of freedom.
And the king landed in Tzitzifies, with epaulets and a dark
beard, very dark. They called him Ras Poupounabi.

Στὸν ὦμο του καθόταν μιὰ κοκκινόκωλη μαϊμού, δεμένη μὲ χρυσὴ
καδένα στὸ κουμπὶ
τοῦ σακακιοῦ του, καὶ μὲ τὸ ζερβί του χέρι κρατοῦσε ἕναν πράσινο
παπαγάλο·
κι ἦταν ξιπόλητος, κι ἐμεῖς ξιπόλητοι φωνάζαμε «Δόξα καὶ δύναμη
στὸ βασιλιά μας τὸ μεγάλο!»
Ἔπειτα ὁ βασιλιάς, ὁ παπαγάλος κι ἡ μαϊμοὺ πῆραν θριαμβικὰ
τὴν ἀνηφόρα·
ταμποῦρλα καὶ λαλούμενα, πέταλα ἀλόγων καὶ κραυγὲς — θά
'λεγες σιδερένια καὶ μπρούντζινη μπόρα
ποὺ σάρωνε τὴ λεωφόρο Συγγροῦ καὶ τρύπωνε μέσα σὲ παρδαλὲς
ἀψίδες:
τὰ φλάμπουρα σύννεφο στὸν οὐρανό, σὰ βαφτισμένες στὶς χίλιες
μπογιὲς ἀκρίδες.
Καὶ τράβηξε ἡ πομπὴ τὸν ἀνήφορο καὶ στάθηκε σ' ἕνα μεγάλο στύλο.
Ἐκεῖ ἦταν κρεμασμένο τὸ σκουτάρι τὸ βασιλικὸ σκαλισμένο σὲ
πολύτιμο ξύλο
ἀπὸ τρεῖς τεχνίτες ξακουστοὺς ποὺ μῆνες μελέτησαν τὶς νέγκρικες
αἴθουσες τοῦ Βρετανικοῦ Μουσείου
καὶ πάνω στὸ σκουτάρι, τὸ πατρογονικὸ ρητὸ ποὺ ἔλεγε μὲ χρυσὰ
γράμματα: «ΔΙΑ ΒΙΟΥ».
Πήδηξε βλέποντας ὁ βασιλιὰς κι ἀπιθώνοντας τὴ μαϊμού, τὸν
παπαγάλο καὶ τὰ σκουτιά του,
εἶπε νὰ παίξουν τ' ἄργανα γιὰ νὰ χορέψει καὶ νὰ καταλάβουμε τὴ
χαρά του.
Δὲν ἦταν χορὸς ἦταν σίφουνας, χάβρα οἱ φωνὲς κι ὁ ρυθμὸς
τραμουντάνα
μανιάζοντας στὴ ράχη τῆς λεωφόρος Συγγροῦ καὶ τὴν ἔδερνε καὶ
τὴν ἐκοπάνα
κι ἔτρεμε ἡ δύστυχη μὲς στὸ βραχνὰ καὶ βόγκαε καὶ λόγιαζε πὼς
θὰ βούλιαξε ἡ χτίση...
Αὐτὸ εἶναι τ' ὄνειρο, Φαβρίκιε. Δὲν ξέρω πότε ὁ δρόμος μας θὰ
ξυπνήσει.

25.11.1935

On his arm sat a red-assed monkey, bound with a gold watch chain to a button
on his suit coat, and with his left hand he held a green parrot.
And he was barefoot and we were barefoot too, shouting, "Glory and power to our great king!"
Next the king, the parrot, and the monkey climbed the hill triumphantly.
Drums and musical instruments, horses clip-clopping, and shouting: It sounded like a thunderstorm of iron and brass,
scraping against the pavement and making holes in crumbling arches,
while pennants filled the sky like clouds, clouds colored by a thousand locusts.
And the procession climbed the hill, stopping at a large pillar.
There hung the royal crest sculpted out of precious wood
by three well-known artisans who spent months studying the Negro art galleries of the British Museum.
And above the crest, the ancestral credo was written in gold letters: "FOR LIFE."
Seeing it, the king jumped for joy, and setting aside his monkey, parrot, and his coat,
he ordered the instruments to play so that he could dance and we could grasp his joy.
It wasn't a dance, it was a tornado, a shouting din, and a rhythm like the north wind,
a mania upon the back of Syngrou Avenue, beating and thrashing her.
The poor thing trembled in the thunder and groaned, afraid that the structure would collapse—
That's the dream, Fabrice. I don't know when our road will wake up.

November 25, 1935

Γιὰ ἕνα διαθέσιμο τριαντάφυλλο

(Γραμμένο μὲ τὸ μολύβι)

Τὸ χωματένιο αὐτὸ σκαμνὶ τ' ἀγόρασα τὴ μέρα τῶν μυροφόρων,
μὲ τὴ σκέψη πὼς ἂν τελειώνει τὸ κορμὶ πάντα ἀπομένει ἡ δίψα
σ' ἕναν προφυλαγμένο χῶρο σὰν ἕνα χθόνιο λιβάδι.
Αὐτὸ ποὺ μᾶς βαραίνει εἶναι ἡ δίψα τῶν ἄλλων, τῶν ἀλλαγμένων·
τοὺς πηγαίνουμε λουλούδια κάθε πρωὶ ξεγελώντας τὸν ἑαυτό
μας —
τί νὰ τὰ κάνουν τὰ λουλούδια; Καὶ ἀνασαίνουν τὰ κυπαρίσσια
κι ἀνάμεσό τους ἐκεῖνα τὰ μάτια.
Ὕστερα ξαναπηγαίνουμε στὶς δουλειές μας· τὰ καράβια
πρέπει νὰ ταξιδεύουν, νὰ φεύγει ἡ γῆς ἀνάμεσα στοὺς δυό της
ὕπνους.
Ποιὸς ξύπνησε σήμερα πρωί; κανείς· μόνο μιὰ γυναίκα
ἔσυρε τὸ χέρι πάνω στὸ γυμνὸ βυζί της καὶ χαμογέλασε·
ἐκεῖνοι ποὺ διψοῦν τὴν κράτησαν στὰ βελουδένια τους σπίτια —
τί νὰ τὰ κάνουν τὰ λουλούδια, καὶ τοῦτο τὸ βυσσινὶ τριαντάφυλλο,
μέσα στὸ χωματένιο σταμνὶ τῶν μυροφόρων, τί νὰ τὸ κάνουν;

Κορυτσά, 26.4.1937

For an Available Rose

(Written in Pencil)

I bought this clay pot on the Sunday of the myrrh-bearers,
while thinking that even when the body is finished,
the thirst remains in a protected place,
like a meadow in the underworld.
What weighs upon us is the thirst of others, of those who have
changed form.
We bring them flowers every morning: a self-deception—
What can these flowers do for them?
The cypress trees breathe and between the trees, those two eyes.
Afterward we go back to work; the ships
must sail, so that the earth can retreat, between her two sleeps.
Who awoke this morning? No one; only a woman
who ran her hand along her naked breast and smiled.
Those who thirst keep her in their velvet houses—
What can they do with flowers? And this cherry-red rose,
inside the clay pot of the myrrh-bearers, what can it do?

Korçë, April 26, 1937

Μεγάλο Σάββατο

Αὔριο Λαμπρή. Βρέχει ἀλλὰ δὲ θά 'χουμε γραφεῖο.
Τ' ἀρνιά, στὸ φοῦρνο, μοῦ θυμίζουν ἕνα ἀπέραντο βρεφοκομεῖο.

Κορυτσά, 1.5.1937

Holy Saturday

Tomorrow, the brilliant light of Easter. It will rain, but at least
we won't be in the office.
The lambs, in the oven, remind me of a huge nursery.

Korçë, May 1, 1937

Selva oscura

Τὰ μάτια ἂν κλείσω βρίσκομαι σ' ἕνα μεγάλον ἴσκιο
τὸ χρῶμα τῆς αὐγῆς τὸ αἰσθάνομαι στὰ δάχτυλά σου.
Ξέχασε τὸ ψέμα ποὺ σὲ βόηθησε νὰ ζήσεις
γύμνωσε τὰ πόδια σου, γύμνωσε τὰ μάτια σου,
μᾶς μένουν λίγα πράγματα ὅταν γυμνωθοῦμε
ἀλλὰ τὰ βλέπουμε στὸ τέλος πιστά.
Τὰ μάτια ἂν κλείσω βρίσκομαι πάντα σ' ἕνα μονοπάτι,
τ' αὐλάκια χαλασμένα δεξιὰ κι ἀριστερά, στὴν ἄκρη
τὸ σπίτι μὲ γυαλιὰ ποὺ τὸ χτυπάει ὁ ἥλιος, ἄδειο.
Σκέφτηκα τὰ δάχτυλά σου νὰ χτυποῦν τὰ τζάμια
σκέφτηκα τὴν καρδιά σου νὰ χτυπᾶ πίσω ἀπ' τὰ τζάμια
καὶ πόσα λίγα πράματα χωρίζουν ἕναν ἄνθρωπο
ποὺ δὲν τὰ ξεπερνᾶ.
Δὲν ξέρεις τίποτε γιατὶ κοίταξες τὸν ἥλιο.
Τὸ αἷμα σου στάλαξε στὰ μαῦρα φύλλα τῆς δάφνης
τ' ἀηδόνι, περασμένες νύχτες, μάρμαρα στὸ φεγγάρι
καὶ στὸ ποτάμι τό 'συρα κι ἔβαψε τὸ ποτάμι.
Συλλογίζομαι, ὅταν συλλογίζομαι, συλλογίζομαι
τὶς φλέβες μου καὶ τὸ μυστήριο τῶν χεριῶν σου ποὺ ὁδηγοῦν
κατεβαίνοντας προσεχτικὰ σκαλοπάτι τὸ σκαλοπάτι[.]
Τὰ μάτια ἂν κλείσω βρίσκομαι σ' ἕναν μεγάλο κῆπο[.]

[Μάης 1937]

Selva Oscura

When I close my eyes, I find myself in an expansive darkness
the color of dawn; I sense it on your fingertips.
Forget the lie that helped you live.
Bare your feet, bare your eyes—
very few things remain when we've bared ourselves
but in the end we can see them exactly as they are.
When I close my eyes I always find myself on a path,
the yards ruined to the right and left and in the corner
the house with windowpanes beaten by the sun, empty.
I thought of your fingertips beating against the panes.
I thought of your heart beating behind the panes
and the very few things that set a man apart from others
and are never overcome.
You don't know anything because you looked at the sun.
Your blood dripped into the black leaves of the laurel bush.
I see the nightingale and the marbled moon of evenings past,
when I dragged your blood into the river, dyeing it red.
I ponder—when I ponder—I ponder
my veins and the mystery of your hands,
guiding carefully, descending step by step.
When I close my eyes, I find myself in an expansive garden.

May 1937

Τὸ ἄλογο τῆς Μολδοβλαχίας

(Σχεδίασμα τοῦ Μαθιοῦ Πασκάλη)

Ἕνα λοφίο μιὰ λόγχη ἕνα δέντρο·
στὴν ἄλλην ὄχθη τὸ ἄλογο.
Ἀνάμεσα κυλᾶνε σάρκες καὶ ἀρώματα γυναικῶν
ἄντρες μαζὶ μὲ τὶς σάρκες, μήτε πρόσχαροι μήτε κατηφεῖς
ἀποφασισμένοι
ὄχι ἀποφασιστικοί,
ἀποφασισμένοι ἀπὸ τοὺς ἄλλους
ἀπὸ τοὺς δυὸ βασιλιάδες ἴσως —
τὸν ἕναν ποὺ κατοικεῖ τὸ μπρούντζινο ἀποτύπωμά του
τὸν ἄλλον ποὺ κατοικεῖ τὸ σάρκινο ἀποτύπωμά του —
ἀπὸ τοὺς δυὸ βασιλιάδες ἴσως
ἢ τὸ ἄλογο
μὲ τὸ βάραθρο τῆς κοιλιᾶς τόσο ἀνάλαφρα ὑψωμένο
πάνω στὰ τέσσερα πόδια
ποὺ μᾶς ἐξαπατοῦν νυχοπατώντας.
Τὸ φοβερὸ δὲ φαίνεται ποτέ·
δὲ φαίνεται τὸ μέγα ἀγκίστρι ποὺ ψαρεύει ἀπὸ τὸ κοκκινωπὸ
    βάθρο·
ὅταν προσέξεις ἀντικρίζεις τὸ χαμό·
τὸ γαντζουρωτὸ σπέρμα
ποὺ τινάζεται ἀπὸ τὰ φριχτὰ ἀχαμνά του
βαριὰ σὰν ἀδιάφορο κανόνι σ' ἀρχοντικὸ τῆς Ὕδρας,
σπόρο θανάτου
ποὺ καρφώνει ἀλάθευτα τὸν ὅποιον σημαδέψει
καὶ τὸν σέρνει καθὼς ὁ Ἀχιλλέας τὸν Ἕκτορα
ἀνάσκελα μέσα στὴ σκόνη
χλωμὸ γυμνὸ ντροπιασμένον
μέσα στὶς κεντητὲς ρεκλάμες ποὺ ἀνάβουν καὶ σβήνουν
μέσα στοὺς κουρασμένους μηροὺς τῶν γυναικῶν
αὐλάκια τοῦ ἔρωτα τελματωμένα·

The Danubian Principalities' Horse

a caprice by Matthew Paschalis

A slope, a spear, a tree;
on the other side, a horse.
In the space between flow bodies, women's fragrances,
men, neither joyful nor glum,
decided
rather than decisive.
Perhaps the others decide for them,
the two kings—
the one inhabiting a bronze form
and the other who inhabits a flesh form.
Perhaps the two kings decide,
or the horse.
His chasm of a belly is so lightly elevated
on four legs;
the sound of his feet clip-clopping on the pavement excites us.
The horror is never revealed;
we never see the great fishhook catching us from the rusted
  red pier;
when you notice terror's presence, you also catch sight of death.
A hook-shaped sperm
bursts forth from his petrifying testicles
and resounds deeply, like an indifferent cannon at a stately
  home in Hydra.
This seed of death
never fails to embed itself in those who are marked;
they are dragged like Achilles did Hector,
on his back, in the dust,
pale, naked, humiliated,
past embroidered and flickering neon signs,
past women's exhausted breasts,
love's stagnate ditches,

μέσα στὰ πυρωμένα λάστιχα καὶ τοὺς ἀχνοὺς τῶν
αὐτοκινήτων
καθὼς βαραίνει ἡ ζέστη κι οἱ στολὲς παρουσιάζουν ὅπλα κι οἱ
μικρὲς μπρούντζινες σάλπιγγες μεῖναν ἀνάερες —
τὸν φέρνει σίγουρα στὴν κοιλιὰ τοῦ ἀλόγου
μὲ τὴν τερατώδη ἀπόφυση τοῦ νεκροῦ βασιλιᾶ στὴ ράχη
καὶ τὰ ρουθούνια του ποὺ ἀνοιγοκλοῦν ἀνασαίνοντας ἀηδία.

Τελετὴ ἀθόρυβη ἀνάκουστη
προσφορὰ στὸν ἄνθρωπο ποὺ κρατοῦσε τὴ σφαίρα καὶ τὸ
σκῆπτρο
προσφορὰ στ' ἄλογο μέσα στὸν ἄνθρωπο ποὺ χλιμιντρᾶ καὶ
ματώνει τὰ νύχια
καὶ δὲ χορταίνει μήτε τώρα ποὺ ὁ ἀναβάτης μετάλλαξε τὸν
ὕπνο
τελετὴ χωρὶς ἱερατικὸ βάδισμα μήτε δαυλοὺς μήτε ἱερουργίες
ἀλλὰ μὲ τὰ καθημερινὰ φερσίματα, τὰ μικροσκοπικὰ παθήματα
καὶ τὶς ἀπρόσωπες χαρές μας,
μὲ τὴ συνηθισμένη ρυτίδα στὸ μέτωπο καθὼς σηκώνεις τὸ
τηλέφωνο ποὺ σημαίνει
μὲ τὸ κουρασμένο μάτι καὶ τὴν ξεβιδωμένη χειραψία ὅταν
συναπαντήσεις κάποιον
ἄρρωστη πομπὴ μὲ τὴν τάξη τοῦ πρόσκαιρα σκηνοθετημένου
κόσμου.

Βουκουρέστι, 19.5.1939

through burning tires and automobile exhaust,
through oppressive heat and military regiments presenting their
weapons, while bugles hover.
Surely the dead are returned to the belly of the horse,
even while the dead king also rides on the horse's back, a
monstrous lump.
And the horse's nostrils flare in revulsion.

A ritual unfolds, soundless and unknown,
an offering to the man who held the globe and scepter,
an offering to the horse within the man;
the horse whinnies and bloodies his hooves,
unsatisfied even now that the rider has alchemized sleep.
A ritual unfolds, devoid of priestly movements, no torches, no
official rites,
rather, a ritual done in our pedestrian ways, with our micro-
afflictions
and impersonal joys,
our brow furrowed as usual when we answer the ringing
phone,
with our tired eyes and handshake jerky when we meet
someone—
a sick procession held in the temporary, staged world order.

Bucharest, May 19, 1939

Le cheval n'a pas dit "M.E.R.D.E."

Μούντζωσ' τα, Τάκη Παπατζώνη, μούντζωσ' τα!
άλλιώτικο ἦταν τ' ἄλογο: λυγρό,
λυγρὸ θὰ τό 'λεγε ὁ Τυφλὸς
ποὺ γνώριζε τὰ ζὰ καὶ τοὺς ἀνθρώπους
καὶ τὸν καθημερνὸ κίνδυνο τῆς ζωῆς.
Τ' ἄκουσες, λές, νὰ σοῦ μιλάει γαλατικὰ
γιὰ τὴν κερα-Εὐρυδίκη ἢ τὸν Καμβρόνη
σὰν τὸ συνταγματάρχη τῆς Τρανσυλβανίας
μὲ τὰ γυαλιστερὰ κουμπιά, τ' ἀμφιμασχάλια
καὶ μὲ ὄνομα (προπάντων) ἑλληνικό,
φυτὸ τῆς λάσπης τοῦ Βυζαντίου.

Αὐτὸ δὲ μίλησε: σὲ γέλασαν.
Τίποτε· τσιμουδιὰ τὸ ἐπικατάρατο,
τὸ ἐπίβουλο, τὸ σόι τοῦ ἐπιβήτορα·
μόνο ἕνας γερο-σάτυρος πιωμένος
ποὺ ἔβγαινε ἀπ' τὴν Bodega Dragomir
μὲς στοὺς βορβορυγμοὺς τῆς βιολογίας του
τὰ πέντε γράμματα τῶν Γαλατῶν ὑποτονθόρυζε.

Βουκουρέστι, Μάης 1939

The Horse Didn't Say "S.H.I.T."

It's a shit show, Taki Papatsonis, screw it!
The horse had changed: devastating,
absolutely devastating, as the Blind Poet would say;
he knew of mice and men
and the everyday risks of life.
You might think you heard the horse
speaking in Gaulish about Madame Eurydice or General
  Cambronne,
as if he were a Transylvanian colonel
with shiny brass buttons, gold braiding around his shoulders,
and a Greek name (above all else),
a weed from the mud of Byzantium.

But he didn't speak: he fooled you.
Zilch—an accursed silence.
What a crafty bastard, scion of the usurper.
He's just an old, drunk satyr
leaving the Bodega Dragomir tavern
with his intestines rumbling full of gas
while muttering St. Paul's five pleas to the Galatians.

Bucharest, May 1939

Μιὰ μελανιὰ στὸ πράσινο στουπόχαρτο,
ἕνα σβησμένο στίχο χωρὶς κατάληξη,
ἕνα φτερὸ ἀπὸ τὸν ἀνεμιστήρα τοῦ καλοκαιριοῦ
ποὺ ἔσπασε κόβοντας τὴν πηχτὴ ζέστη·
τὴ ζώνη ποὺ ἔμεινε στὰ χέρια μου
καθὼς ὁ πόθος πέρασε στ' ἄλλο ἀκρογιάλι —
αὐτὰ μπορῶ νὰ σοῦ χαρίσω, Περσεφόνη,
κι ἐσὺ λυπήσου με καὶ δῶσε μου μιᾶς ὥρας ὕπνο.

[Ὀκτώβριος 1939]

A bruise on green blotting paper,
an erased stanza, no climax,
a blade of summer's fan
that broke while slicing thick heat;
the belt that remained in my hands
while desire passed to the other shore—
these things I can grant you, Persephone,
and you, have mercy on me
and give me one hour of sleep.

October 1939

Τοῦτο τὸν ἀναπτήρα ἀνάγλυφο
σ' ἕνα κομμάτι μάρμαρο τῆς Μάνης,
Παφία, σοῦ τὸν χάρισε ἡ Βιττώ,
τώρα ποὺ ξέρει πὼς δὲ γνώρισε τὴν ἡδονή:
τοὺς ἄλλους ἄναψε, ποτὲ τὸν ἑαυτό της.

[Ὀκτώβριος 1939]

This lighter in bas relief
on a piece of marble from Mani,
was dedicated to you, Aphrodite Paphia,
by the maiden Vitto.
Now she realizes she never knew pleasure:
it lit the others, but never herself.

October 1939

Ἦταν ἕνας νέος στὴν Ἀντιόχεια
πού 'λεγε μόνος: «Ἀντίο; Ὄχι, ἄ-
βριο μπροστὰ στὸ πλοῖο
θὰ σοῦ πῶ στ' ἀλήθεια ἀντίο
σένα ποὺ μ' ἔμπλεξες στοῦ ἡδονισμοῦ τὰ βρόχια».

2.10.1941

There was a young man from Antioch
who merely said: "Goodbye—no,
tomorrow on the pier
I will truly bid you farewell, dear,
you who tangled me in hedonism's snares."

October 2, 1941

[Προμετωπίδα σὲ μιὰ ἀντιγραφὴ τῶν «Ὠδῶν»]

«Θλίβει ὁ καπνὸς τὸ διάστημα γαλάζιον τῶν ἀέρων…»
    — διαβάζω
Κάλβο, ποὺ τύπωσε στὰ ’26 καὶ τὸν γνωρίσαμε στὰ ’88·
καὶ ποὺ ἔμεινε ἀξομολόγητος στὰ γεροντάματα, σὰν ἕνα
    «ραγισμένο βάζο»,
στὰ χέρια μιᾶς γριᾶς Ἐγγλέζας δασκάλας, σύμβολο
    ἀκατάλυτο καὶ φριχτὸ

γιὰ ὅσους ἐπιμένουν νὰ γράφουν στίχους ἢ πρόζα ποὺ κανεὶς
    δὲν καταλαβαίνει,
καὶ γυρεύουν νὰ δοξαστοῦν, οἱ τυχάρπαστοι, ἀπὸ τοὺς
    λογάδες καὶ τοὺς σοφούς,
ἐνῶ θὰ νά ’ταν χίλιες φορὲς προτιμότερο, καὶ ἡ τέχνη πολὺ
    πιὸ εὐτυχισμένη,
ἂν πήγαιναν στὴν Ἐκάλη νὰ μαζεύουν κούμαρα, ἢ στὴ
    Γλυφάδα νὰ ψαρεύουν ροφούς.

Τράνσβααλ, 11.12.1941

Frontispiece to a Facsimile of Odes by Andreas Kalvos

I read—*the smoke saddens the entire expanse of the blue sky*—
Kalvos, although printed in 1826, was unknown to us until 1888.
He remained mum in old age, like Prudhomme's "cracked vase"
in the hands of an elderly English governess. A symbol,
awesome and wide,

for those of us who insist on writing lines no one understands,
and who seek praise—darn upstarts—from rhetoricians and
the wise
though we'd be more successful and we'd prefer it a thousand
times
if we went to Ekali for berries or Glyfada to catch fish with
our hands.

Transvaal, December 11, 1941

Τὸ ἄλλοθι
ἤ
Ἐλεύθεροι Ἕλληνες, '43

Στὰ νερὰ τοῦ Τάμεση
στὰ νερὰ τοῦ Νείλου
ἔνιβε τὰ χέρια του
κι ἔλεγε: δὲν εἶμ' ἐγὼ
κι ἔλεγε: δὲν εἶμ' ἐγώ.

The Alibi
or
Free Greeks, 1943

In the waters of the Thames,
in the waters of the Nile,
he cleansed his hands
and said: I'm not myself
and said: I'm not myself.

Ἀντάρτες στὴ Μ.Α.
(Ἀφήγηση γιὰ τὰ παιδιὰ)

Ἥσυχοι ἤμασταν, ἂς ποῦμε,
ἐδῶ πού ’λαχε νὰ ζοῦμε
μὲς στὴ ζέστη τὴν ὑγρὴ
μὲς στὴ Μέση Ἀνατολή.
Φούσκωνε καὶ τὸ ποτάμι,
φούσκωναν καὶ τὰ μυαλὰ
κι ἤμασταν σὰν τὸ καλάμι
στὴν παχιὰ ἀκροποταμιά.
Ὅταν ἤρθανε οἱ ἀντάρτες
μὲ πιστόλες καὶ μὲ χάρτες
νὰ ταράξουν τὴ ζωή μας.
Ἦρθε ὁ Ροῦκος, ἦρθε ὁ Ντύμας,
ὁ Κατάρλης μὲ τὸν Πύρο,
κι ὁ Δεσπότης μὲ τὸν Τζίρο,
καὶ τοὺς βάλαν στ’ ἀψηλὰ
μὲ χαφιέδες καὶ δροσιὰ
νὰ θυμοῦνται τὰ βουνά.

«Τί γυρεύουν; Τί γυρεύουν;»
φώναζαν στὶς παροικίες.
«Τί γυρεύουν; Τί γυρεύουν;»
φώναζαν στὶς νταχαμπίες.
«Ποιὸς τοὺς ἔφερε δῶ-πέρα
νὰ μᾶς πάρουν τὸν ἀέρα;»
«Μὴν τοὺς φέραν οἱ Σύμμαχοι;»
«Ἀλλ’ αὐτοὶ μᾶς ἀγαποῦν
καὶ δὲ θέλουν τὴν ἀμάχη
στοὺς λαοὺς ποὺ πολεμοῦν
γιὰ νὰ ζήσει ἡ ἀνθρωπότη
ἔξω ἀπ’ τῆς σκλαβιᾶς τὰ σκότη».
«Μὴν τοὺς φέραν οἱ Ἀραπάδες

Partisans in the Middle East
(A Recounting for the Guys)

Things were quiet, let's say,
here where fate decreed we stay
in the heat festering like yeast
within the Middle East.
When the river began to swell,
our minds expanded as well
like the rushes, in ranks
thick, on the riverbank.
It was then that the partisans
landed with pistols and maps,
no more business as usual.
Dimas was with Roukos,
Katarlis with Pyro,
and the Boss with Tsiro.
To remind them of Greece,
they were put on fresh peaks
where spies lurked in deceit.

"What've they got going on?
What've they got going on?"
they said in the colonial haunts.
"Who are they trying to wile?
Who are they trying to wile?"
they said, dining on the Nile.
"We wonder, to whose avail
would it be to send these males
to take the wind from our sails?"
"Maybe it was the Allies?"
"But it's us they prize
and enmity they abhor
among the peoples at war

γιὰ νὰ πάρουνε μπαξίσι;»
«Ἀδερφέ μου, οἱ Ἑλληνάδες
ποὺ γλεντοῦν σὲ κάθε κρίση,
αὐτοὶ πάλι βρῆκαν κάτι
νὰ μᾶς κόψουν τὸ ραχάτι».

Κίτρινος καὶ σιωπηλός,
ὅταν τὸν ρωτήσουν κάτι,
μ' ἕνα νεκρωμένο μάτι
τοὺς κοιτάει καὶ τοὺς ρωτᾶ:
«Ποῦ τὰ βρήκατε ὅλα αὐτά;
Τί 'ναι αὐτὸς ὁ λουκουμάς;
Ἄρτζι μπούρτζι καὶ λουλάς,
πράσινα ἄλογα καὶ θειάφι,
δὲν τ' ἀφήνετε στὸ ράφι
μὲ μιὰ τρύπια κατσαρόλα,
μ' ἕνα πράσο, μὲ μιὰ φόλα —
μολονότι ὀρθὸν θὰ ἦτονα
νὰ ρωτῆστε καὶ τὸ γείτονα,
νὰ ρωτῆστε τὸ χασάπη,
νὰ ρωτῆστε τὸν ἀράπη
ποὺ πουλάει ζεστὰ σουδάνια
καλοχώνευτα καὶ σπάνια».

Οἱ ἀντάρτες σὰν τὸν εἶδαν
πῆγε νὰ τοὺς φύγει ἡ βίδα.
Μέρα-νύχτα συζητοῦσαν,
μέρα-νύχτα πολεμοῦσαν,
γιὰ νὰ βροῦνε κάποια λύση
στῆς Ἀνατολῆς τὴν κρίση
πού ἦταν πιὰ μασκαραλίκι.
Μὰ οἱ Ἐγγλέζοι ποὺ τοὺς θρέφαν
χωρὶς νὰ πλερώνουν νοίκι,

to rescue humanity
from the evil of slavery."
"Maybe it was the Arabs, though,
wanting to make a little dough?"
"But friend, what about the main-
land Greeks? They do acclaim
with joy each crisis and pain.
They must have found a cause
to interrupt our restful pause."

Whenever they would pry
he was slow to reply.
Sallow, with a cold eye,
he'd ask: "What kind of nonsense
is this? I've lost the thread.
You're talking horse sense.
Why don't you put it on a shelf,
it'd be much better for your health;
idle talk is a poison to the self.
Instead, it would be proper
to inquire of your neighbor
and your local butcher
and the Arab in his stall
offering warm peanuts to all.
It'd be a lot easier to swallow."

When the partisans laid eyes
on their nation's prized
figurehead, they realized
the severity of their plight.
They negotiated, day and night,
they battled, day and night,
to solve the crisis in our land
that had become a total sham.
Instead, the Brits who fed
this beast but paid not a red

ἔπαψαν νὰ παίζουν πρέφα
καὶ σὰ νὰ μοιράζαν κόλλυβα
τοὺς ἐμάζεψαν ἀθόρυβα
καὶ τοὺς στείλανε ξανὰ
στὰ ψηλά τους τὰ βουνά.

«Τὰ Περιστέρια»
5.9. – 24.10.1943

cent for its upkeep, decided
to call trump on their friends.
Without giving an explanation,
as solemn as a funeral oration,
they gathered up the partisans,
and off they went again
to the high mountains.

"The Doves"
September 5–October 24, 1943

Χορικὸ ἀπὸ τὸν «Μαθιὸ Πασκάλη Δεσμώτη»
(Παστίτσιο)

Κάτω ἀπ' τὸ δέ-, κάτω ἀπ' τὸ -ντρό,
μωρ' πῶς τὸν τρώει, μωρ' πῶς τὸν τρώ-,
κάτω ἀπ' τὸ δέντρο τοῦ μπαμποὺ
ἀκούστη μπάμ, ἀκούστη μπούμ,
κι ἀπὸ δέκα μεῖναν τρεῖς,
μωρ' πῶς τὸν τρίβει, πῶς τὸν τρί-,
κι ἀπὸ τρεῖς ἀπόμειν' ἕνας:
δέκα, τρεῖς, παρακανένας.

Κεῖ ποὺ ἀνθίζει ἡ τζακαράντα
κι ἀρμενίζει μὲ μιὰ μπάντα
ἡ φελούκα στὸ νερὸ
σὰ νεγρέσα γκαστρωμένη,
κάτω ἀπ' τὸ δέ-, κάτω ἀπ' τὸ -ντρό,
κάτω ἀπ' τὸ δέντρο τοῦ μπαμποὺ
ἀκούστη μπάμ, ἀκούστη μποὺμ
καὶ βρεθήκανε χεσμένοι.

Μοῦτρο λαίμαργο σὰ φώκια
στὸ Ζαμάλεκ καλαμπόκια
θά 'ρθουν πάλι γιὰ νὰ φᾶς
θά 'ρθουν καὶ ζαχαροκάλεμα
νὰ μασήσεις σὰν πεινᾶς.
Δὲν κοιτᾶς τὸ χαροπάλεμα
τόσου κόσμου καὶ τὰ χάλια μας;
Πάψε νὰ χτυπᾶς τὴ γλώσσα
πάψε νὰ γυρνᾶς σὰν κλώσα
πού είναι δίχως κλωσοπούλια
μὲ τὸν ἥλιο ἢ μὲ τὴν Πούλια
κάτω ἀπ' τὸ δέντρο τοῦ μπαμποὺ
μέσα στὸ μπάμ, μέσα στὸ μπούμ.

Chorale from Matthew Paschalis, Prisoner of War

A Pastiche

Under the tr-, under the -ee,
child, he is destroyed, child he is destroy-ed.
Under the babul tree
a bam, a boom, suddenly
out of ten remained three.
Child, he is wiped out, scraped.
And then out of three remained one:
ten, three, not even a soul.

There where the jacaranda flowers
and a small fleet anchors,
a felucca plies the Nile,
like an African woman swelling with child.
Under the tr-, under the -ee,
under the babul tree
a bam, a boom, suddenly,
we've shit ourselves.

A piggish face like a seal,
like a corn cob from Zamalek,
will come again to feed you.
When you're hungry, they'll be back
with only sugarcane to champ.
Don't you see the multitudes
battling death and our misery?
Stop flapping your tongue,
stop circling like a hen with no brood
day and eve under the babul tree,
with a bam and a boom.

Στὸ Ζαμάλεκ δὲς μιὰ βίλα
ὅπου τὰ φλογάτα φύλλα
σὰν τὴ γλώσσα τοῦ λικόρνου
γλείφουνε τὸν ούρανό,
έκειπέρα τοῦ κοθόρνου
τὸ μυστήριο έρευνῶ·
πῶς ψηλώνει τοὺς άνθρώπους
χωρὶς ἵδρωτα καὶ κόπους
καὶ πῶς τοὺς τρώει καὶ πῶς τοὺς τρώ-,
χωρὶς πίκρες καὶ μεράκια,
καὶ βυθίζουν τὰ γεράκια
κάτω άπ' τὸ δέντρο τοῦ μπαμπού,
μέσα στὸ μπάμ, μέσα στὸ μπούμ.

Sh. Emad el Din, 6.5.1944

There's a villa in Zamalek
where the crimson leaves
are like a unicorn's tongue,
licking the heavens.
I want to know the secrets
of their ancient cothurnus boots.
How they elevate the wearer
without sweat and elbow grease,
and then are destroyed—
without sorrows and passion,
they are destroyed.
The falcons sink into the horizon
under the babul tree,
with a bam, with a boom.

Emad El-Din Street, Cairo, May 6, 1944

Τὸ ἀπομεσήμερο ἑνὸς φαύλου

Τράβα ἀγωγιάτη, καρότσα τράβα,
τράβα νὰ φτάσουμε γοργὰ στὴν Κάβα!
Φύσα βαπόρι, βόα μηχανή,
νὰ 'ρθοῦμε πρῶτοι ἐμεῖς! — οἱ στερνοί.

Τὰ στερνοπαίδια καὶ τ' ἀποσπόρια
καὶ τ' ἀποβράσματα καὶ τ' ἀποφόρια
μιᾶς μάχης ποὺ ἤτανε γι' ἄλλα κορμιὰ
γιὰ μάτια ἀλλιώτικα κι ἄλλη καρδιά.

Πολιτικάντηδες, καραβανάδες,
ψιλικατζῆδες, κολλυβιστάδες,
μοῦργοι, μουνοῦχοι καὶ θηλυκὰ —
τράβα ἀγωγιάτη! βάρα ἀμαξά!

Φτωχὴ Πατρίδα, στὰ μάγουλά σου
μαχαίρια γράφουνε τὸ γολγοθά σου·
μάνα λιοντόκαρδη, μάνα ὀρφανή,
κοίτα ἂν ἀντέχεις τέτοια πομπή:

τὸ ματσαράγκα, τὸ φαταούλα
μὲ μπογαλάκια καὶ μὲ μπαοῦλα·
τὴ χύτρα ποὺ ἔβραζε κάθε βρωμιὰ
λὲς καὶ τὴν ἄδειασαν ὅλη μεμιὰ

σ' αὐτοὺς ἀνάμεσα τοὺς ἤπιους λόφους
ὅπου μᾶς κλείσανε σὰν ὑποτρόφους
ἑνὸς ἀδιάντροπου φρενοβλαβῆ
ποὺ στὸ βραχνά του παραμιλεῖ.

Δὲς τὸ σελέμη, δὲς καὶ τὸ φάντη
πῶς θυμιατίζουνε τὸν ἱεροφάντη

Afternoon of a Faun

Drive coachman, click clack!
To Cava, without any slack!
Ferry puff, motor crack!
Let us get there first,
we who hung back.

Johnny-come-latelies and the last-in-lines,
the dregs and hand-me-downs
of a conflict designed
for other bodies, hearts, and eyes.

Politicos, small-timers, and carnies,
loan sharks, bumpkins, eunuchs, and sissies—
Pull this cart, burn rubber!

Our poor homeland, the lashes
on your cheeks reveal your ordeal.
Lionhearted mother, orphaned mother,
see if you can handle this bunch:

the racket runner, the greedy pig
with bundles and hoards.
Imagine the spew from a stinky,
simmering brew dumped in a rush

on top of us, in the soft hollows
where we were held as wards
of a brazen crackbrain, hoarse,
howling in his delirium.

Look at the freeloader, look at the rascal,
how they blow smoke up the cleric's asshole

πoὺ ρητορεύεται λειτουργικὰ
μπρὸς στὰ πιστά του μηρυκαστικά.

Μαυραγορίτες ἀπὸ τὰ Νάφια
τῆς προσφυγιᾶς μας ἄθλια σινάφια,
γύφτοι ξετσίπωτοι κι ἀρπαχτικοί,
λένε, πατρίδα, πὼς πᾶνε ἐκεῖ

στὰ χώματά σου τὰ λαβωμένα
γιατὶ μαράζωσαν, τάχα, στὰ ξένα
καὶ δὲν μποροῦνε χωρὶς ἐσὲ —
οἱ φαῦλοι: τρέχουνε γιὰ τὸ λουφέ.

Cava dei Tirreni, 7.10.1944

while he bloviates his liturgical words
before the faithful ruminating herd.

NAAFI black marketeers,
our exile's sinister syndicate,
gypsies, stinting snatchers,
making claims of ennui

supposedly, homeland, they're speeding
to your blood-soaked earth, depleted
and they can't go on without you—
the fauns: chasing after loot.

Cava de' Tirreni, October 7, 1944

Χωρὶς χρῶμα, χωρὶς σῶμα
τούτη ἡ ἀγάπη ποῦ πηγαίνει
σκορπισμένη, μαζεμένη,
σκορπισμένη πάλι-πάλι,
κι ὅμως σφύζει κι ὅμως πάλλει
στὴ δαγκωματιὰ τοῦ μήλου
στὴ χαραματιὰ τοῦ σύκου
σ' ἕνα βυσσινὶ κεράσι
σὲ μιὰ ρώγα ἀπὸ ροδίτη
τόση ἀνάερη Ἀφροδίτη,
θὰ διψάσει θὰ κεράσει
ἕνα στόμα κι ἄλλο στόμα
χωρὶς χρῶμα, χωρὶς σῶμα.

28.8.1945

No color, no shape
the kind of love that
dissipates, melds,
and dissolves again.
Yet it pulsates and dashes
in the apple's gash,
in the fig's scar,
in a crimson cherry,
in a pink-skinned grape,
a dappled nipple.
For the sake of
impalpable Aphrodite
mouth after mouth
will thirst and be slaked,
no color, no shape.

August 28, 1945

Κυπρίς, γιὰ τὴν ἀγάπη σου πολὺ βαθιὰ βυθίσαν
καὶ τὰ πουλιὰ καὶ τὰ κεράσια καὶ τ' ἀστέρια
καὶ τὰ ψαράκια τοῦ γιαλοῦ ποὺ τόσο μὲ βοηθῆσαν
νὰ κυνηγήσω τὸ λαγό σου μὲ τὰ δυό μου χέρια.

27.5.1946

Cyprian Aphrodite, for the sake of your love
the birds, the cherries, the stars above,
and the little fish along the shore sank
into the depths of the ocean dank.
All this helped me to catch your hare
with my bare hands.

May 27, 1946

Παλεύανε τὰ χείλια ἀποζητώντας, γιὰ νὰ ξεδιψάσουν,
τὸ δροσερὸ λιβάδι ποὺ τὸ πότιζε ὁ Εὐρώτας,
κι ἐσὺ καβάλα στὸ λαγωνικό σου κάλπαζες μὴ σὲ προφτάσουν
κι ἀπὸ τὶς ρῶγες τῶν βυζιῶν σου στάλαζε ὁ ἱδρώτας.

[Ἰούνιος 1946;]

Anguished lips, thirsty with craving, quiver,
a fresh meadow cooled by love's river.
Rider, you drove your bloodhound so raw and quick—
breasts slick with sweat as you gave them the slip.

June 1946?

Ἡ Κυρία Ζὲν

ΔΙΑΒΑΤΗΣ: *Κούφια καρύδια· τί τὰ μαζεύεις;*
ΜΑΘΙΟΣ: *Θέλω νὰ φτιάξω ἕνα ἀνθρωπάκι.*
ΔΙΑΒΑΤΗΣ: *Γερο-ξεκούτη, δὲν τὰ παρατᾶς; σήκω*
καὶ πράξε κάτι χρήσιμο.

Contrattempo, senza brio

Ἔμεινα χτὲς τ' ἀπόγεμα
μόνος στὴν κάμαρά μου·
τὰ ἐπίπονα χαρτιά μου
μ' εἶχαν κουράσει πιά.
Κι ἔτσι, ἀδειανός, ἀκούμπησα
στ' ἀνώφελο τραπέζι
κοιτάζοντας νὰ παίζει
μιὰ μύγα, νευρικά,

στὸ τζάμι ποὺ μὲ χώριζε
ἀπὸ τὸ φρέσκο ἀγέρα
καὶ ζάρωνε τὴ μέρα.
Στὸ φῶς τοῦ δειλινοῦ
τὰ πεῦκα τόσο ἀνήσυχα
θυμίζανε τὰ χέρια
ψάχνοντας περιστέρια
τὴ νύχτα ἐκείνη, ποὺ

ἀγκάλιασα ἀναπάντεχα
σ' ἕνα φριχτὸ κρεβάτι
ποὺ φώτιζε ἡ Ἑκάτη
τὸν Ἔρωτα νεκρό.
Τὰ δάχτυλά μου παίζανε
μ' ἕνα κούφιο καρύδι
καὶ μ' ἕνα βαλανίδι

Mrs. Zen

PASSERBY:	*Empty walnut shells—for what?*
MATTHEW:	*I want to make a little figurine.*
PASSERBY:	*You're off your rocker, old man. Leave them be.* *Get up and make something useful.*

Contrattempo, senza brio

At sunset yesterday,
alone I stayed. Thorny
paperwork had completely
flattened me. And so, empty,
upon my useless desk I leaned

watching a fly on the screen,
playing the space between
me, the fresh air, and the light
which was shrinking into night.
The sunset seemed to incite
an anxiety in the pines.
Their branches reminded me of
hands searching for doves,
a sudden terror, on that night

when I found in my embrace
that Love had died, by the grace
of torch-bearing Hekate.
My fingers played idly
with a hollow walnut shell,
and a smaller one as well,
plus an acorn, dallying

κι ἕν' ἄλλο πιὸ μικρὸ
καὶ κάτι βέργες ποὺ ἔκοψα
μαζὶ μ' ἕνα καλάμι.
Σὰ χταποδιοῦ θολάμι
ὁ νοῦς σιγὰ-σιγὰ
ἔνιωθε τὸ ξετύλιγμα
τῶν πλόκαμων ν' ἀνοίγει,
ν' ἁπλώνει, νὰ τυλίγει
ἕνα σῶμα, κρυφά,

τὰ λυγισμένα γόνατα
τὸ κοιμισμένο δέρας.
Δυνάμωνε ὁ ἀγέρας·
ἡ σκέψη μου ρηχὴ
χαμήλωνε χαμήλωνε
ὅλο πρὸς τὰ κοχύλια,
τὰ χαραγμένα χείλια,
τὴν κλειστὴ μουσικὴ

κι αὐτὰ τὰ μικροπράγματα
ποὺ μὲ τὰ δάχτυλά μου
ταίριαζα, καὶ μακριά μου
χανόντουσαν, καὶ δὲν
ἀπόμενε πιὰ τίποτε
παρὰ λίγο φαρμάκι
καὶ τοῦτο τ' ἀνθρωπάκι
ποὺ λέω Κυρία Ζέν.

Πόρος, 26.10.1946

with some branches that I cut
together with a rush.
Like an octopus's murky
ink the mind gradually
unwound its kinks,
no more need to think,
an unknown rhythm, weaving
a body in secret, conceiving,

a weakness in the knees
awakened a dormant fleece.
The wind picked up speed.
My thoughts in the weeds
grew deeper and deeper still,
closer to the shells, the trill

of inner sounds, etched
lips, pieces that suited
my fingers. Slowly they drew
away from me and grew
fainter until nothing else
remained but a healing pulse
and this tiny person
whom I call Mrs. Zen.

Poros, October 26, 1946

Ὁ Δρ Ρώτλαουφ καὶ ἡ Κα Ζὲν

Ὁ Δρ Ρώτλαουφ καπνίζει τὸ τσιγάρο του κοιτάζοντας τὸ κανάλι
τοῦ Πόρου
ἡ Κα Ζὲν εἶναι πολὺ προκλητική, δημιούργημα τῆς φαντασίας
ἑνὸς ἀπόρου.

Ὁ Δρ Ρώτλαουφ ἔριξε πίσω τὸ καπέλο του κι ἀκουμπᾶ τὸ
μπαστούνι του σ' ἕνα στρείδι
ἡ Κα Ζὲν ἀπειλεῖ νὰ σπαράξει τὸ ντουνιά· τὸ κεφάλι της εἶναι
τρύπιο καρύδι.

Ὁ Δρ Ρώτλαουφ, μὲ μάτια μύωπα, κοιτᾶ στ' ἀποβράσματα τῆς
θάλασσας, πράγματα παράξενα καὶ κάποτε σπουδαῖα
ἡ Κα Ζὲν κρατάει σκουτάρι καὶ σπαθί· φορεῖ μιὰ θυσανωτὴ
περικεφαλαία.

Ὁ Δρ Ρώτλαουφ εἶναι ἄμεμπτος· τὸ παλτό του καμηλό, τὸ
τσιγάρο του Παπαστράτου 2
ἡ Κα Ζὲν (εἶπε ἡ χαρτοὺ) πρέπει νὰ βγάλει μάτι γιὰ νὰ βρεῖ τὸν
ὀμορφονιὸ ποὺ θὰ τὴ ζεσταίνει στὸ κρύο.

Ὁ Δρ Ρώτλαουφ πηγαίνει ἀνύποπτος, χαζός, συνεπαρμένος
ἀπὸ τὰ ψάρια ποὺ χοροπηδοῦνε —
Μάδησε μιὰ μαργαρίτα, Μαθιέ!... Θὰ συναντηθοῦνε;... δὲ θὰ
συναντηθοῦνε;... θὰ συναντηθοῦνε;...

Πόρος, 31.10.1946

Dr. Rothlauf and Mrs. Zen

Dr. Rothlauf watches the Poros canal while smoking a cigarette
and Mrs. Zen is a very provocative creature who emerged from
a pauper's mindset.

Dr. Rothlauf throws down his hat and leans his cane on a
barnacle.
Mrs. Zen threatens to tear the world to pieces; her head is a
cracked walnut shell.

Dr. Rothlauf, nearsighted, looks at sea scum, strange yet
meaningful stuff.
Mrs. Zen holds a lance and shield; she wears a helmet with
tufts.

Dr. Rothlauf is impeccably dressed; in a camel overcoat, he
smokes Papastratos 2s, those cigarettes of old.
Mrs. Zen (the paper said) obviously must find a handsome
man who will keep her warm against the cold.

Dr. Rothlauf goes along clueless, dumb, mesmerized by the
jumping fish, how neat—
Pluck a daisy's petals, Matthew!... Will they?... Or won't
they?... Will they meet?

Poros, October 31, 1946

Ἀριάδνη

Ἦταν ὡραῖα τὰ χείλια σου καὶ σ' ἄρεσε ἡ ἐλιὰ
ποὺ δάγκωσες· τὸ κόκκινο, τὸ πυρρό, καὶ τὸ μαῦρο
σμίγουν καλὰ σὰν ἁπλωθεῖ τὸ χέρι στὴ θελιὰ
κι ἀφήσει ἐλεύθερο τὸ σκύλο, τὸ λαγό, τὸν ταῦρο.

Καὶ λάμπουνε τὰ ζῶα ζεστὰ στὴ μέρα τὴν κλειστὴ
κι ὅλα μαζὶ πλοκάμων κόμποι καὶ σφιγμένα μέλη,
δόντια σὲ δυὸ βατόμουρα, καὶ θάμνοι ἀγκαθεροί,
καὶ δάχτυλα χαϊδεύοντας τὸ φῶς σὰν ἕνα χέλι

χρυσό, ποὺ τρύπησε τὸν ἄσπρο θόλο τ' οὐρανοῦ —
κι ὅλα μαζὶ λικνίζουνται στὴν ἄκρη τῆς ἀβύσσου,
χωρὶς ἐγώ, χωρὶς εἱρμό, κι οἱ κορφὲς τοῦ βουνοῦ
ποὺ ξύπνησαν τόσο σκληρές· καὶ τὸ γλυφὸ κορμί σου

χορεύοντας, πεθαίνοντας, χορεύοντας ξανὰ
καὶ τὸ καλάμι καρφωμένο στ' ὀργισμένο δέλτα...
...βαθύ... πουλί... χιμῶ... λαβή... τυφλή... λαβώ... λαβ... λα...
...βύρινθος... ἄλφα... βήτα... γάμα... δέλτα...

Πόρος, 3.11.1946

Ariadne

As you bit the olive, how beautiful were your lips!
Two reds—cherry and flame—merge in full
with black, when the hand upon the leash slips
and releases the dog, the hare, and the bull.

The animals shine in daylight, replete and warm,
braided knots, limbs an intertwined swarm,
a thorny bush, two raspberries, bitten.
Fingers stroking the light like a golden

eel that pierced heaven's ivory vault—
on the edge of the abyss, they rock gently.
No I, no coherence, the mountain tops
awakened abruptly. Your briny body

dancing, dying, dancing again,
a reed nailed to the engorged delta.
Deep—bird—I burst—grip—blind—I wound—la—
lab—byrinth—alpha—beta—gamma—delta—

Poros, November 3, 1946

Ὠδὴ
εἰς μιξοκάλβειους στροφὰς

πρὸς τὸν
εὐσεβέστατον, ἐμβριθέστατον,
προσηνέστατον
ὀτρηρὸν τῶν Μουσῶν θαλαμηπόλον
κύριον
Τάκην Παπατζώνην,
συνταχθεῖσα
ὑπὸ
Ματθαίου Πασκάλη
τοῦ ἐπιλεγομένου
παρά τισιν ἀνιδέοις καὶ ἐλαφροῖς
Ἐγκλείστου τοῦ Πεπορωμένου,
ὑποψηφίου διὰ τὸ ἔπαθλον Νόβελ,
ἐν Πεπόρῳ, Νοεμβρίου ΚΣΤ΄
τοῦ σωτηρίου ἔτους ͵ΑϠΜΣΤ΄

Κατέβα, ὦ Πάν! Καὶ σὺ Πρίαπε
τοῦ καλαμαρίου, ἐλθέ! Νύμφαι
τῶν πεύκων κρυφθῆτε! Τώρα θὰ ὑμνήσω
τὸν Παπατζώνην!

Ὅπως ὁ ναύτης, μετὰ πολλὰς Ἰθάκας
καὶ ναυάγια, φθάνει εἰς τὴν ὄχθην
ὅπου προσμένει κρονόληρος πατὴρ
καὶ κατεβαίνει

μαζί του εἰς τὸν ὑπόγειον τάφον
νὰ προσκυνήσει κάρας προγόνων·
ἔτσι στρέφω τὰ νῶτα στὴν φθινοπωρινὴν
ἰσημερίαν.

Ode
In Bastardized Verse à la Kalvos

Dedicated to
The Most Revered, Most Profound,
Most Affable
Hardworking Butler to the Muses,
Sir
Takis Papatsonis,
Composed
By
Matthew Paschalis,
Chosen
On Account of Ignorance and Frivolity
To Be a Prisoner of Fate,
Nominee for the Nobel Prize,
Theoretically, on November 26,
In the Year of Our Lord 1946

Descend, o Pan! And you Priapus,
of the reed flute, come! Maidens
of the pines, abscond! Now I shall sing a paean
  to Papatsonis!

Like a sailor landing on the shore
after many Ithacas and shipwrecks
and a father, battered by time's fracas,
  waits and descends

with him, to a subterranean grave
genuflecting to the ancestral relics.
Just as now, I revolve and flank
  the autumnal equinox.

Ὁ πείσμων γέρων μὲ τὰς δασώδεις
ὀφρῦς καὶ τὸ ἀργυροῦν ρεῦμα τοῦ πώγωνος,
ἄχυμος, παγερός, τυφλὸς τὸν νοῦν καὶ τὰ ὄμματα,
κυφὸς ἐμπρός μου,

μὲ σύρει ἐν μέσῳ ἀρπακτικῶν
τρωκτικῶν μὲ βλέμμα πολιτευομένου
παμπόνηρον καὶ τὴν ούρὰν
σὰν τριπιτσόνι.

Φεύγει τὸ ριγηλὸν πέλαγος
ὡσὰν τὸ κυανοῦν πτερούγισμα
τῆς Ἀλκυόνος, καὶ τοῦ παρθένου κύματος
ἡ συνουσία

φεύγει, ἀνελήφθη, καθὼς
κύπτω τὸν θλιβερὸν αὐχένα μου
στὸ σκοτεινὸν ἀνώφλι
μὲ μαύρας σκέψεις.

Τί μ' ἀπομένει; Ποῦ θέλω εὑρεῖν
παρηγορητικὸν ἐλιξίριον;
Σὺ τὸ κατέχεις, πάροικε τοῦ εὐγενοῦς
Κολωνακίου!

Πτωχὸς ὁ βίος, πορνικὸς
ὡσὰν τὸ κεκμηκὸς γύναιον
τῆς Τρανσυλβανίας πάλλει
μπλὲ βλεφαρίδας·

χασμᾶται καὶ ὀνειρεύεται
ἐν ἐγρηγόρσει πράξεις
πανούργους καὶ μιαρὰς
καὶ ψυχοφθόρους.

The stubborn old man stoops before me sapless,
indifferent, benighted and blind,
with eyebrows thick as a forest and a
    silver-streaked beard.

He pulls me into a nest of grasping
rodents with the look of a consummate
trickster and a tail spiraling like a
    corkscrew.

Trembling in flight, the sea recedes before
me like the cyan wings of the halcyon.
So too the virgin wave as it meets the shore
    in intercourse

ebbs, and is assumed, while I
crane my sad neck
toward the shadowy threshold,
    with dark thoughts.

What recourse? Where can I find
a healing elixir? You must have it,
alien of the race
    of Kolonaki!

This poor life, whorish
like the little woman
of Transylvania, flaps
    its blue eyelids.

It yawns and dreams
in quick movements that are
cunning and contagious
    and soul-crushing.

Δὲν μὲ τρομάζει, μήτε
θέλω δειλιάσειν, ἀφ' οὗ
ΣΥ μένεις στὴν ταράτσαν σου
    πιστὸς εἰς τ' ἄστρα!

Ἄγε, λοιπόν, ἄδραξον
τὴν Λύραν καὶ τὸν Στέφανον,
Φίλε, καὶ δῶσε με λέξεις
    ἐσταυρωμένας!

I fear not, though,
nor do I desire to be affrighted
since you remain on your patio
    trusting in the stars!

Come, therefore, Friend,
harness the Lyre and the Crown,
and give me words
    with the sign of the cross!

Ἐλεγίσκος

Τὸ κονυζόχι, τὸ θυμάρι, τὴν ἀφάνα
καὶ τὸ κυκλάμινο ποὺ γίνεται μὲ τὸν καιρὸ πιὸ σκοῦρο
καὶ τὸ βουνὸ ποὺ παίρνει χρῶμα δαγκωμένο μοῦρο
τὸ δειλινὸ —
Ὦ Μοῦσες! Μοῦσες, θὰ τὸ ξαναϊδῶ;
Ἀοιδή! Μελέτη! Μνημοσύνη!
Πότε θὰ δείξει ἡ Ἀλκυόνα καλοσύνη;
Πότε θὰ ξαναϊδῶ τὴ Μαγκουφάνα;

8.10.1948

Elegiac

Fleabane, thyme, brushwood: these
and the cyclamen that darkens by degrees
and the mountain that blushes
like a bitten mulberry
as the sun dips below the trees—
O Muses! Muses, will I ever see it again?
Aoede! Melete! Mnemosyne!
When will Alcyone grant her favor?
When will I see Athens's megafauna again?

October 8, 1948

Τί εἶπε ἡ γκαμήλα

(Παστίτσιο)

...Κάθισα σ' ἕνα πάγκο χαζεύοντας
Τάχα θὰ 'ρθεῖ κανεὶς γιὰ πασατέμπο
Τὰ κόκκινα μῆλα, τὰ πράσινα φύλλα μ' ἀρέσουν πολύ,
  μ' ἀρέσουν πολὺ
«Κάθε ποὺ πέφτουν τὰ μεσάνυχτα τὸ λύνω»
Πότε θὰ πιάσω τὸ κοτσύφι — Ὦ κότσυφα, κότσυφα
«Ἐνθάδε κεῖται Ταρσεὺς μὴ γήμας»
Μὲ τὰ στραγάλια αὐτὰ πέρασα τ' ἀπόγεμά μου.
«Ἔχω ἀκατάλυτα μαλλιὰ καὶ δόντια». Πάλι μαλακίζεται
  ὁ μπαγάσας.
Evlendirelim. Nerede bulalım. Suradan buradan bulalım.
Tamam Tamam Tamam.

[1948;]

What the Camel Said

A Pastiche

I was lolling fruitlessly on a bench—
shall anyone come by with pumpkin seeds?
I do like melons and peaches, yes, I do.
"When midnight comes, I let my hair down."
When will I catch that braid? O blackbird blackbird.
"Here lies Tarseus, unmarried."
With these salted nuts I have spent my afternoon.
"I might be old, but my teeth and hair endure."
He's jerking off again, the slippery bastard.
Evlendirelim. Nerede bulalım. Suradan buradan bulalım.
Tamam Tamam Tamam.

1948?

Μπχαμντοὺν

Χτυπᾶ ἡ καρδιὰ
γρήγορα-γρήγορα
αὐτὰ τὰ βουνὰ
μᾶς μοιάζουν σίγουρα.
Γρήγορα-γρήγορα
ψάχνεις νὰ βρεῖς
τὸ γνώριμο χορὸ
μιᾶς φωτεινῆς
πλαγιᾶς ποὺ φόρεσε
ξάφνω τὸ δείλι·
χτυπᾶ ἡ καρδιὰ
τρέμουν τὰ χείλη —
Κι ἐδῶ μᾶς γέλασαν
γρήγορα-γρήγορα·
Φοίνικες ἔμποροι
πουλοῦσαν εἴδωλα,
δὲν ἦταν βουνά.

Ξενοδοχεῖο «Ambassadeurs»
27.8.1953

Bhamdoun

The heart beats
speedily. These
mountains, certainly,
resemble ours.
An abrupt desire,
hoping to spy
the familiar dance,
a sudden brilliance,
sunset on the steeps.
The heart beats,
lips shiver—
palms and peddlers
wasted no time
with their deceits.
Instead of peaks,
they sold us fantasies.

Ambassadors Hotel
August 27, 1953

Ντοὺρ έλ Σουὲρ

Πεῦκα χωρὶς ἀνάσα, κι ἂς εἶναι τόσα.
Δῶθε ἀπὸ τὸ Σκορπιὸ στοῦ Γαλαξία τὰ κρόσσια
χτυπᾶ ἡ καμπάνα·
ἀπὸ μπακίρες τῶν Σελευκιδῶν
πρέπει νὰ φτιάξαν αὐτὸν τὸν ἦχο.
Ἐκεῖ ποὺ τὸ λαγκάδι γίνεται ρηχὸ
οἱ αἰσθήσεις βρίσκουν κάποτε ἕναν τοῖχο
ἀπὸ νεκρὰ τριζόνια.
Τὸ ράδιο τραγουδᾶ παθητικὰ
ὁ σκύλος κουρεμένος προσεχτικὰ
πηδᾶ καὶ τρέμουν τὰ ποτήρια·
τὸ κρύο γυαλὶ φέρνει τὴ μνήμη σὲ βιτρίνα
ἑνὸς παλιοῦ μουσείου.
Καθὼς ἀκοῦς τὸν ἄλλο ποὺ σὲ προσφωνεῖ «Μουσιού»,
τὴ Συροφοίνισσα ποὺ βιάζεται νὰ τὸν βασκάνει,
θὲς νὰ φωνάξεις: «Θεέ μου, τί ἔχουν κάνει;
μ' ἔκλεισαν κατὰ λάθος ἐκεῖ μέσα
μὲ τὶς μπακίρες τῶν Σελευκιδῶν!»

«Ὀρτέντσιες» 14.9.1953

Dhour El Choueir

A multitude of pines, a breathless swell.
The ringing of a bell;
it resounds from the stars of Scorpio to the galaxy's rim.
Such a bell brims
with the tone of bronze coins from the Seleucids.
Where the ravine shallows and skids
the senses meet resistance—
a wall of dead insects.
The radio sings, unmoved.
The dog is carefully groomed;
he jumps and rattles the glass,
triggering the memory of an old museum case.
When someone calls you *"Mus-you,"*
and then a Syrophoenician woman, *tout a coup,*
lances him with the evil eye,
you want to scream: "Oh my,
what have they done?
They shut me up in here, shunned,
mistakenly joined with the Seleucids' coins!"

Hotel Hortensias, September 14, 1953

Ταξίδεψα κουράστηκα κι ἔγραψα λίγο
μὰ συλλογίστηκα πολὺ τὸ γυρισμό, σαράντα χρόνια·
σ' ὅλες τὶς ἡλικίες ὁ ἄνθρωπος εἶναι ἕνα βρέφος,
ἡ τρυφερότητα κι ἡ κτηνωδία τῆς κούνιας·
τ' ἄλλα τ' ἀποτελειώνει ἡ θάλασσα σὰν τ' ἀκρογιάλι,
τὴν ἀγκαλιά μας καὶ τὸν ἦχο τῆς φωνῆς μας.

[1954;]

I wandered, got tired, wrote very little.
But returning home was always on my mind—40 years.
Man is an infant at all ages—
in the cradle's tenderness and brutality.
Like the shoreline and the sea, everything else is erased—
our embrace and the sound of our voice.

1954?

Έξι ρίμες γιὰ δώδεκα μαχαίρια

Στὴ Λένα καὶ τὸν Γιῶργο Σαββίδη

α΄

Πάνω σὲ κάμα δίκοπη θὰ γράψω τ' ὄνομά σου
νὰ τὴν καρφώσω στὴν καρδιὰ μὲ τὴν κορμοστασιά σου.

β΄

Μὴν τὰ πετᾶς τὰ λόγια σου σὰν τ' ἄχερο στ' ἀλώνι·
μοῦ 'καμες πέτρα τὴν καρδιὰ κι ἡ κάμα σου στομώνει.

γ΄

Χώρισα τὸ ροδάκινο μὲ τοῦτο τὸ μαχαίρι
πὼς μ' ἄνοιξες τὸν κόρφο σου στὸν ἥλιο μεσημέρι.

δ΄

Κοπέλα μαυρομαντιλού, μὴν παίζεις μὲ τὰ ψάρια
μπορεῖ μαχαίρια νὰ γενοῦν καὶ σφάζουν παλικάρια.

ε΄

Λεπίδι ποὺ μὲ χτύπησες, ἤσουν τὸ νέο φεγγάρι
στὴ γέμισή του κόκκινο στὴ χάση του κουφάρι.

στ΄

Τὸ δαφνόφυλλο ἄστραψε σὰν ἀναμμένο βάτο,
ὁ ἐχτρὸς τὸ καταράστηκε κι ὁ φίλος εὐλογᾶ το.

Ἀμοργός, 4.9.1961

Six Rhymes for Twelve Knives

for Lena and George Savidis

1

I'll write your name on a double-edged blade
and drive it into the heart of your poised frame.

2

Don't toss your words around like chaff before a flail.
It hardens my heart and as a turn on, it fails.

3

I split your peach with this here blade—
hot in the midday sun, you opened your glade.

4

Girl in black, don't play with the naïfs.
Knives may come out and fell the popinjays.

5

Shiv that slashed me, you were the new moon
waxing, flush with the stiff's crimson bloom.

6

The switch gleamed, a tiny bay leaf that grew into a
bush, burning.
The friend blessed it, while the enemy fell, cursing.

Amorgos, September 4, 1961

Ἀπὸ βλακεία

Ἑλλάς· πῦρ! Ἑλλήνων· πῦρ! Χριστιανῶν· πῦρ!
Τρεῖς λέξεις νεκρές. Γιατί τὶς σκοτώσατε;

Ἀθήνα, καλοκαίρι – Princeton N.J., Χριστούγεννα 1968

Φθαρμένη ἐπιγραφὴ

...Λέξεις νεκρές. Γιατί τὶς σκοτώσατε;...

On Account of Idiocy

Hellas: Let it burn!
Hellenes: Burn!
Christians: Burn!
Three dead words. Why did you kill them?

Athens, Summer—Princeton, NJ, Christmas 1968

A Worn-out Epigram

Dead words. Why did you kill them?

Μότο γιὰ ἕνα ἡλιακὸ ρολόι στὴ Σκαρδαμούλα

Ὅταν τὸ φῶς χορεύει
μιλῶ δίκαια.

[1968;]

Motto for a Sundial in Skardamoula

When the light dances
I speak with equity.

1968?

Τὰ φύλλα τῆς λεύκας γέμισαν ἀναστεναγμοὺς
κι οἱ στεναγμοὶ γέννησαν ἀναστενάρηδες
χάλασαν τὸ δάσος.
Δὲν ἔχουμε πιὰ δέντρα —

The aspen leaves filled with groans
and their moans gave birth to those possessed by fire.
They destroyed the forest.
We no longer have trees.

Καθὼς βαδίζει ὁ χρόνος
καὶ προχωρεῖ ὁ χειμώνας
κι ἡ τραχηλιὰ τοῦ κοκκινολαίμη
στρέφει στὸ πιὸ σκοῦρο
σὰν τὰ κυκλάμινα —

As time marches on
and so does winter,
the robin's red throat
turns ever darker
like the cyclamens.

Καλλιγραφήματα (1941-1942)

Calligraphies (1941–1942)

Ἂν ἀγγίξεις τὴ λύρα
τὰ δάχτυλά σου ματώνουν.
Ὁ Θεὸς δὲν τὸ θέλει.
Καλύτερα νὰ κοιμηθεῖς
στὸν ἴσκιο της.
Ἴσως ἕνα ὄνειρο
παραστρατισμένο
ἔρθει νὰ σ' ἐλεήσει.
Ὅμως, κοίταξε καλὰ
πῶς θὰ στήσεις
τὶς ξόβεργές σου.
Ἂν φτερουγίσουνε τὰ ψάρια
μὴν ξυπνήσεις·
σκέψου πὼς εἶναι
χελιδονόψαρα
ἢ τὰ φτερὰ τοῦ λογισμοῦ σου.

4.10.1941

If you touch the lyre,
your fingers bleed.
God doesn't want it.
Better to sleep
in its shade.
Perhaps a stray
dream will arrive,
taking pity on you.
Use care, however,
when setting up
your traps for the winged ones.
If they should ascend,
don't wake up.
Remember: They are
your thoughts soaring
like flying fish.

October 4, 1941

Τί ἔχασες, δυστυχισμένη
κι ἀφήνεις τὰ μάτια σου
νὰ βρέχουνται καὶ νὰ πνίγουνται
σὰ νά 'ταν νερολούλουδα
μὲς στὴ βροχή;
Μήπως γυρεύεις τὴ θάλασσα
ἢ μήπως εἶσαι ἡ γαλήνη τῆς θάλασσας
δυστυχισμένη;

4.10.1941

What did you lose, sad woman?
Your eyes
rain tears and drown
like a water lily
in the rain.
Perhaps you are longing for the sea
or maybe you, poor woman,
are the serenity of the sea?

October 4, 1941

Ξενιτιὰ ἀνυπόφορη

Ὅταν πονοῦν
οἱ γυναῖκες γίνουνται ἀνυπόφορες
καὶ τὰ σύννεφα βαραίνουν
καὶ τὰ σύννεφα βαραίνουν
καὶ τὰ σύννεφα βαραίνουν χωρὶς
νὰ βρέχει
καὶ αὐλακώνουν τὸν οὐρανὸ
ἀστραπὲς χωρὶς βροντή.
Γιατί μᾶς βασανίζει τόσο
ἡ ἀργοπορία λίγης βροχῆς;
Δυὸ χελιδόνια πετοῦν
ψηλὰ μέσα στὸ δυνατὸν ἀγέρα
μιὰ ἀμαζόνα καλπάζει χωρὶς ἀσπίδα
ὁ κεραυνὸς τῆς ἔκαψε τὴ μήτρα.
Συλλογίζομαι θαλασσινοὺς ποὺ ταξιδεύουν.

4.10.1941

Unbearable Exile

When women are in pain
it is hard to bear
and the clouds hang heavy
and the clouds hang heavy
and the clouds hang heavy without
raining
and silent lightning strikes
hollow the heavens.
Why are we so tortured
by the slow arrival of a little rain?
Two swallows fly
high within the powerful wind,
an Amazon gallops without her shield.
The thunderbolt burned her womb.
I'm contemplating those who are at sea.

October 4, 1941

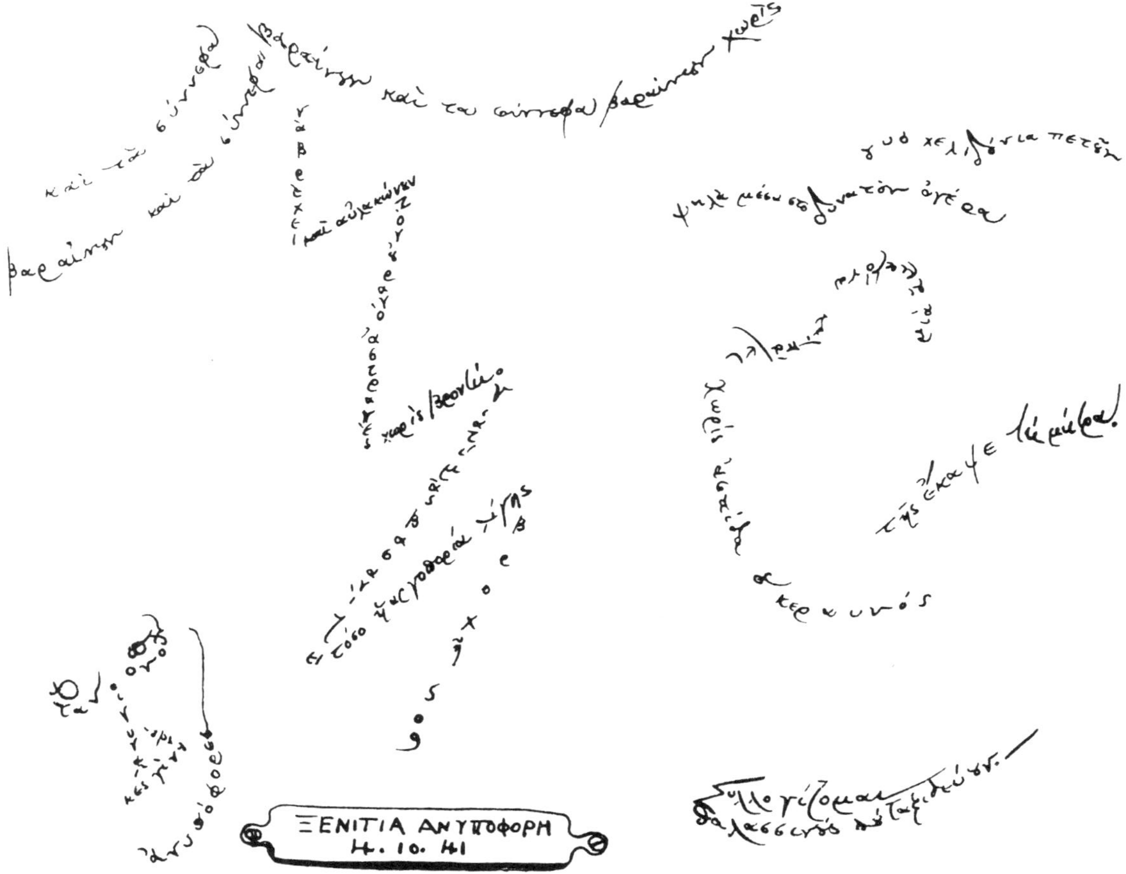
ΞΕΝΙΤΙΑ ΑΝΤΥΠΟΦΟΡΗ
14. 10. 41

Καὶ τὰ λουλούδια βγάλαν μιὰ φωνὴ
τὰ κυπαρίσσια βγάλαν μιὰ φωνὴ
κι ἀπ' τὸ πηγάδι βγῆκε μιὰ φωνή:
Γιατί τοὺς σκοτώνετε;

Ὀκτώβριος 1941

The flowers cried out.
The cypresses cried out.
And a voice rang from the well:
Why did you kill them?

October 1941

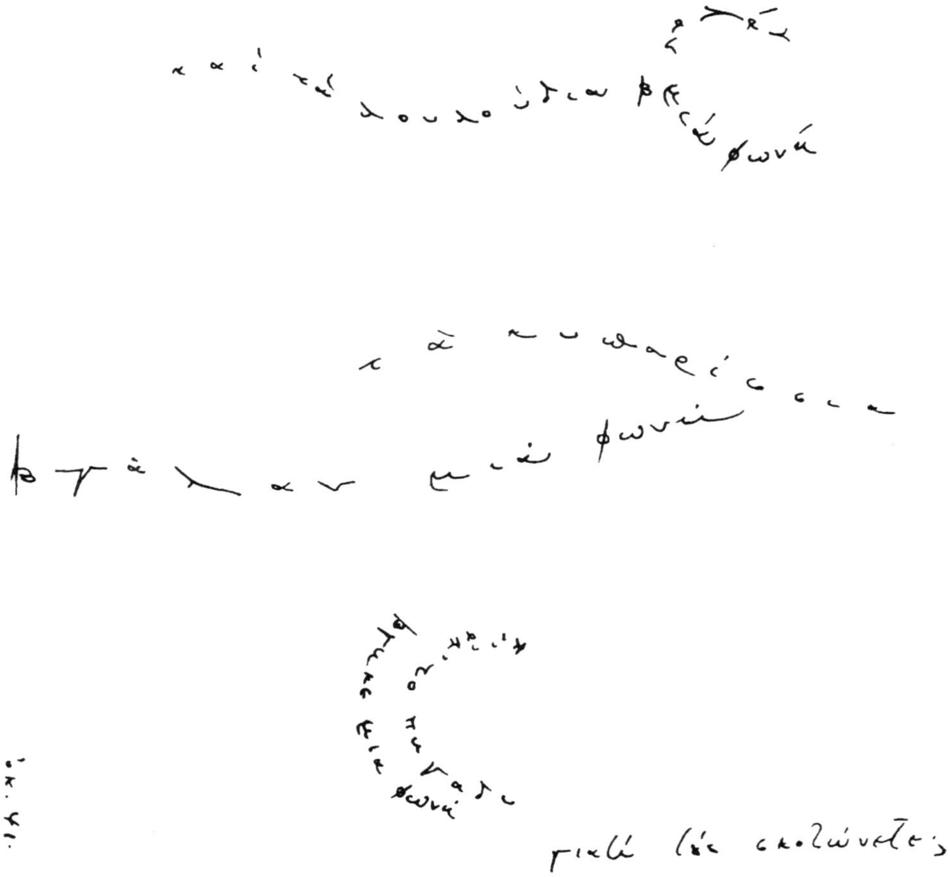
βγάλαν μιά φωνή
γιατί τις σκοτώνετε;
Όκ. 41.

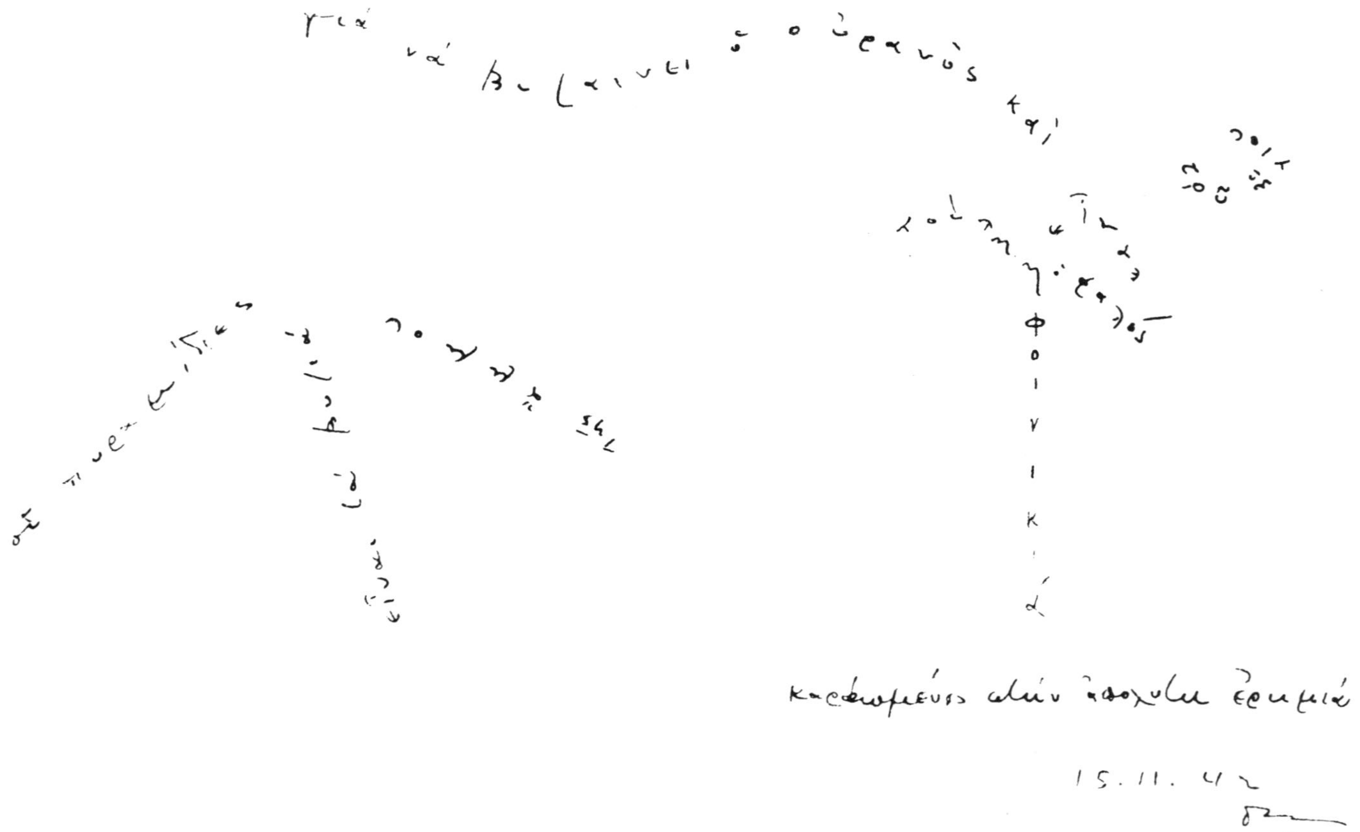
γιά νά βυζαίνει ὁ οὐρανός
φοινικιά
15.11.42

Οἱ Πυραμίδες
εἶναι τὰ βυζιὰ τῆς ἄμμου
γιὰ νὰ βυζαίνει ὁ οὐρανὸς
καὶ τούτη ἡ φοινικιὰ
εἶναι ὁ φαλλὸς τοῦ ἥλιου
καρφωμένος στὴν ἀπόλυτη ἐρημιά.

15.11.1942

The pyramids are
the breasts of the sand,
nursing heaven.
And that palm tree
is the phallus of the sun,
erect in total desertion.

November 15, 1942

Ἐπιδρομὴ

Οἱ προβολεῖς σαρώνουν τ' ἄστρα
σαρώνουν τ' ἄστρα
ἀντένες ἀπὸ μεγάλες κατσαρίδες
ἢ σὰν τὰ δάχτυλα ποὺ σμίγουν
καὶ σταυρώνουνται σὲ στιγμὲς
ἀναμονῆς ἢ ἀδημονίας
ἀποσιωπητικὰ πολύχρωμα
ὢ ὢ ὢ ὢ ὢ ὢ
οἱ τροχιοδεικτικές.

17.11.1942

Air Raid

The projectiles
skim the stars,
skim the stars.
Huge cockroach antennae
or fingers interlaced,
crossed in moments
of waiting or impatience.
Multicolored ellipses,
oh oh oh oh oh oh
the tracer missiles.

November 17, 1942

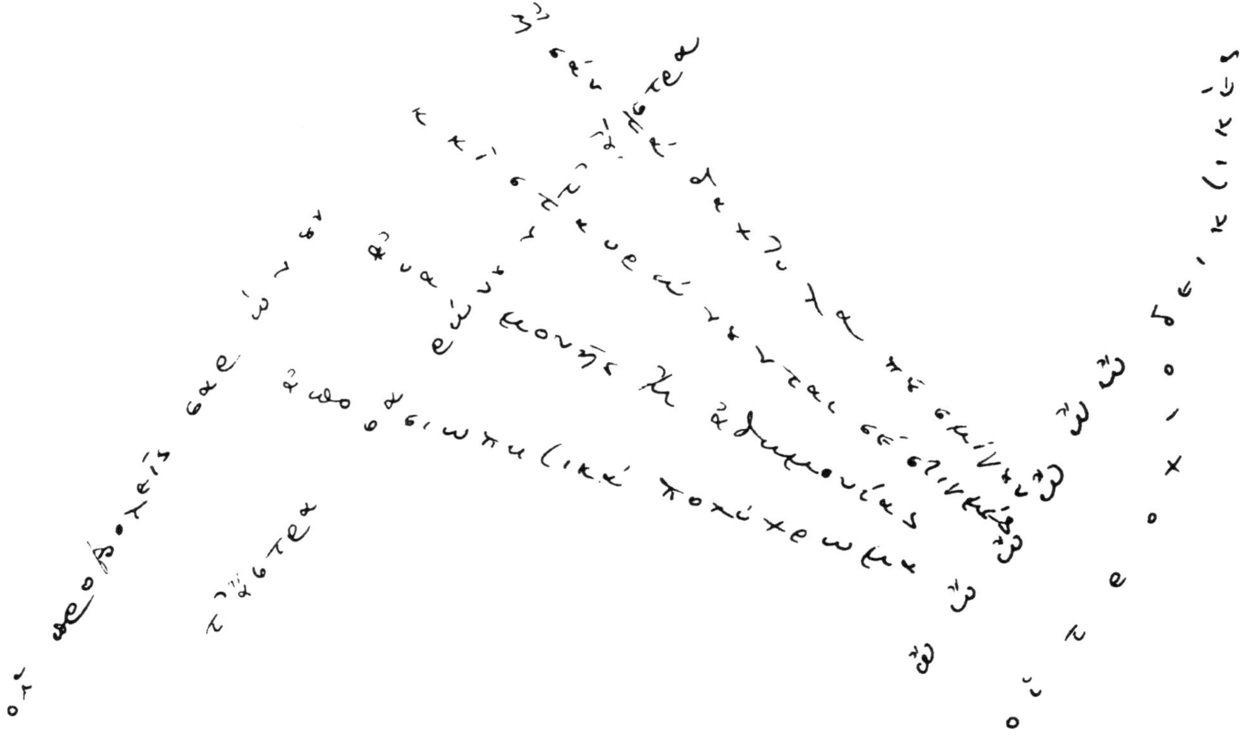

ΕΠΙΔΡΟΜΗ
17.11.42

Notes to the Poems

The Blind Man

This poem refers to the *Dekemvriana* of December 1944, an outbreak of bloody skirmishes between Greek left and right factions, with the British army supporting the right.

"L'Angolo Franciscano"

This was the private name for Seferis's backyard garden at his home in Ankara, Turkey, where he was posted between 1948 and 1950.

Monumentum Ancyranum

Monumentum Ancyranum is an inscription in Latin and Greek on the Temple of Rome and Augustus in Ankara, Turkey (circa 14 AD), which celebrates the life and accomplishments of Roman emperor Augustus. The poem, however, refers to another inscription in the temple dedicated to a Byzantine regiment leader (*tourmarches*) of the ninth or tenth century named Eustathios. Seferis nicknamed him Stathis; his entry for September 4, 1949 in *Days 5* reports that Stathis "had become one of the few good friends Ankara provided."

Letter to Rex Warner

Rex Warner (1905–1986) was an English writer and classicist who served as the director of the British Institute in Athens from 1945 to 1947. His first novel was titled *The Wild Goose Chase.*

The Cats of St. Nicholas

A literary response to the censorship of the Junta dictatorship, this poem was first published in Greece in July 1970 in *Eighteen Texts.* The translation of the epigraph from Aeschylus is my own, but based on Gregory Nagy, Gregory Crane, and Graeme Bird's revisions of the Herbert Weir Smyth English translation.

"On the Aspalathus..."

The quotation refers to Plato's *Republic*, Book 10, 616a (the Myth of Er). Ardiaeus is a tyrant who is tortured in the afterlife, an allusion to the Junta dictatorship's Colonels. Published in the newspaper *To Vima* three days after his death, this was Seferis's last poem.

Indian Folktale

Seferis's original note to this poem: "[Critics] said of *Turning Point* that ... it was 'a book that offers only words.' I attempted to write in accordance with their ideas and I tried out words that were entirely unknown to me. I borrowed them from Lorentzos Mavilis's Greek edition of the *Mahabharata*." In Greek, this poem contains the homonyms *amalakes* (amalaki trees) and *malakes* (assholes).

"This round's on Seferis"

One of several poems drawn from the letters between Seferis and George Theotokas (1905–1966), a fellow member of the Greek Generation of the '30s artists and writers. Fabrice was Seferis's pet name for Theotokas, while *Argo* was the title of Theotokas's 1933 novel. Other poems mentioning Fabrice from the 1930s are "Mr. Lovemaker A. Fatass Dances" and "Syngrou Avenue II."

"At the head, soldiers at arms in uniform and crests"

A draft poem from *Mythistorema*, not included in the finished work; the final three lines are taken from the final lines of Aeschylus's *Eumenides*. *Mythistorema*, published in 1935, is a defining example of Greek modernism and Seferis's personal style. Written in twenty-four poems of free verse, like the *Odyssey*'s twenty-four books, *Mythistorema* offers a fragmented narrative of a displaced Greek collective in a desolate, seaside Greek landscape. There are many direct references to ancient Greek myth and literature, as well as the Asia Minor Catastrophe. "At the head, soldiers at arms in uniforms and crests" and "The Final Chorus" are set in Athens, rather than the generic island landscapes in the published version of *Mythistorema*.

The Final Chorus

A draft poem from *Mythistorema*, not included in the finished work.

Syngrou Avenue II

This is a sequel to "Syngrou Avenue, 1930" in *Collected Poems*. It was sent privately to George Theotokas. Both Seferis and Theotokas were born in Asia Minor and supported the Venizelist, anti-monarchy efforts that exiled King George II in 1924 after the unsuccessful Leonardopoulos-Gargalidis military coup. Political instability and plotting by the royalists led to the restoration of King George II by a rigged plebiscite in the fall of 1935. On November 25, 1935, King George II returned to Athens and was welcomed with a military parade. This poem satirizes the monarch's return through a racially charged comparison between Greece and Ethiopia. For more on this poem's colonial and racial dimensions, see "Emperor Ras Tafari in Piraeus: Seferis's Colonial Anxieties" by Akis Gavriilidis in *Journal of Modern Greek Studies*, 37:2, October 2019.

The Danubian Principalities' Horse

The Danubian Principalities was a name for the regions of Wallachia, Moldavia, and Transylvania, now in Romania, used in both the Hapsburg and Ottoman periods. This poem was written during the Balkan Pact negotiations of 1939, following Italy's invasion of Albania in April of 1939.

The Horse Didn't Say "S.H.I.T."

Takis Papatsonis (1895–1976) was a Greek poet and government official who accompanied Seferis to Bucharest in May of 1939. The horse mentioned in this poem (and the previous one) was a massive bronze equestrian statue of King Carol I sculpted by Ivan Meštrović and installed in front of the royal palace in May of 1939. According to Papatsonis in his essay "Myth and History" from the 1961 book *For Seferis*, during Papatsonis and Seferis's visit the statue was still wrapped in burlap with only its hooves visible. Papatsonis and Seferis joked that this horse was an oracle, like the horse in the Cocteau play *Orphée*, who prophesies Eurydice's death and return by tapping a hoof. While Cocteau's horse conveys an acrostic poem spelling out *merde*, the Romanian horse is mum.

"A bruise on green blotting paper"

This poem and the one that follows are poetic imitations of selections from the *Palatine Anthology*, a collection of ancient Greek poems and epigrams compiled in the Byzantine era.

"There was a young man from Antioch"

This is an attempt at a limerick in Greek. *Book of Exercises II* also contains Seferis's translations of Edward Lear limericks into Greek, which our edition omits.

Frontispiece to a Facsimile of Odes by Andreas Kalvos

Andreas Kalvos (1792–1869) was a Greek Romantic poet. "The smoke saddens the entire expanse of the blue sky" is a quote from Kalvos's ode "To Chios." This poem was written in the front of a notebook where George and Maro Seferis copied Kalvos's *Odes* while in South Africa in 1941.

The Alibi or Free Greeks, 1943

In April 1941, when the Germans invaded Greece, Seferis left Athens and accompanied the Greek government-in-exile to Crete and then Cairo. The figure in this poem is either King George II or Emmanouil Tsouderos, the Prime Minister of the Greek government-in-exile.

Partisans in the Middle East

Satirizes a secret meeting that the British arranged in Egypt between Greek resistance leaders of various partisan factions. Pseudonyms are used for Petros Rousos (1908–1992), Andreas Tzimas (1909–1972), Georgios Kartalis (1908–1957), Komninos Pyromaglou (1899–1980), Konstantinos Despotopoulos (1913–2016), and Ilias Tsirimokos (1907–1968). Roderick Beaton, in *George Seferis: Waiting for the Angel, a Biography*, summarized this event by saying, "[The meeting's] only effect had been to drive the rival groups farther apart, and to make more obvious than ever, to someone in [Seferis's] position, how badly out of touch the exiled government was with its nominal subjects in Greece." "Here Among the Bones" in *Collected Poems* is also about this meeting.

Chorale from Matthew Paschalis, Prisoner of War

This poem is a pastiche inspired by T.S. Eliot's *Sweeney Agonistes*. It satirizes two events from the spring of 1944: a mutiny among the Greek Armed Forces in the Middle East, which lead to their being disbanded by the British and factionalism in Greece that caused three Prime Ministers to be installed during the month of April.

Mrs. Zen

During a vacation to Poros in 1946, Seferis wrote in *Days 5* that he "fashioned a small doll out of a walnut and some acorns, naming her Mrs. Zen." According to George Savidis, the epigraph is a reference to either Confucius or Ezra Pound.

Dr. Rothlauf and Mrs. Zen

Dr. Rothlauf was an anthropomorphic figure made by Seferis from sticks and nut shells, like Mrs. Zen. Dr. Rothlauf was named for a Bavarian doctor who died in an outbreak of the plague in Poros in 1837.

What the Camel Said

A parody of the final part of T. S. Eliot's *The Waste Land*, "What the Thunder Said." Mimicking *The Waste Land*'s style, Seferis's pastiche brings together quotations from the *Palatine Anthology* ("Here lies Tarseus, unmarried") and poets Napoleon Lapathiotis (1888–1944) ("When midnight comes, I let my hair down") and Apostolos Melachrinos (1880–1952) ("my teeth and hair endure"), as well as the staccato sounds of foreign words. Whereas Eliot uses Sanskrit words from the *Upanishads* to express what the thunder said, Seferis uses Turkish words to express what the camel said. I have left the words of the camel in Turkish to evoke *The Waste Land*. The first line in Turkish comes from the novel *Land of*

Aeolia by Ilias Venezis describing the life of the camel driver: "Each camel has its bell, each bell has its sound ... the first sound from the head camel is *Evlendirelim* (Let's get married). The second sound from the second camel more deeply says *Nerede bulalım* (Where can we find it?). And the third sound, severe and slow, joins the first two and responds *Suradan, Suradan* (Over there)." Seferis adds extra text in Turkish: *buradan bulalım* (let's find it here) and *Tamam Tamam* (Okay, fine). Although this poem is undated, it was probably written in 1948 while Seferis was posted to Ankara. My translation of this poem and its note are indebted to Katerina Kostiou's detailed analysis "Ἀπὸ τὴν παρωδία στὸ pastiche: ζητήματα ὁρολογίας καὶ θεωρίας. Μιὰ 'εἰδολογικὴ' προσέγγιση τοῦ ποιήματος 'Τί εἶπε ἡ γκαμήλα (παστίτσιο)' τοῦ Γιώργου Σεφέρη" ("From Parody to Pastiche: Issues of Terminology and Theory. A Typological Approach to the Poem 'What the Camel Said' [Pastiche] by George Seferis") in *Continuities, Discontinuities, Ruptures in the Greek World (1204–2014): Economy, Society, History, Literature: Proceedings of the Fifth European Congress of Modern Greek Studies, Vol II,* edited by Constantinos Dimadis.

On Account of Idiocy & A Worn-out Epigram

These words conclude the essay "Manuscript, Oct. '68" ("Χειρόγραφο Ὀκτ. '68"), finished while Seferis was a visiting scholar at the Princeton Institute for Advanced Study. His time in America coincided with the Junta dictatorship of the Colonels, leaving Seferis in the difficult position of being a former government official now representing his country abroad as a writer. The dictatorship had recently adopted the ideological slogan "Hellas of Christian Greeks" (Ἑλλὰς Ἑλλήνων Χριστιανῶν), which Seferis criticizes here.

Acknowledgments

This project would not have come to life without the essential support of the American Literary Translators Association's Emerging Translators Fellowship, and my mentor Kareem James Abu-Zeid; Katerina Karydi at Ikaros; and the encouragement of Willa Carroll and Mari E. Brown. I am grateful to Spiridon Theodorou for his translation assistance with Greek nautical terms and David Leskowitz with Sanskrit. It is a great joy to publish with World Poetry Books and work with Matvei Yankelevich and Peter Constantine. Special thanks to Glenn Kellogg, Gregory Nagy, and Ioanna Papadopoulou, without whom my work with George Seferis would still be an unrealized dream.

I would also like to thank the editors of *The Common*, *The Kenyon Review*, *AGNI*, *Consequence*, and *Plume* for publishing earlier versions of selected translations.

George Seferis (1900–1971) was a Greek poet, diplomat, and literary critic who won the Nobel Prize in Literature in 1963. As a diplomat for the Greek nation, Seferis served during the Metaxas dictatorship of the 1930s, in exile throughout World War II, during the Greek Civil War and the Cyprus crisis. His death during the Junta dictatorship was a moment of national mourning and resistance.

Jennifer R. Kellogg is a literary translator from Modern Greek and holds a PhD in Modern Languages and Literatures from the Université Libre de Bruxelles (ULB). In 2019 she was an Emerging Translator Mentee of the American Literary Translators Association. Her translations have appeared in *The Common* and *Kenyon Review*.

This book was typeset in Miasma, designed by George Triantafyllakos for Atypical in 2020 to combine the idiosyncrasies of the Apla typeface style of many Greek publications with the strict, upright character of Latin letterforms. The cover of this book features a detail of Yannis Moralis's "Painted Comments," an illustration for the *Poems* of George Seferis published by Ikaros in 1965. Cover design by Andrew Bourne. Typesetting by Don't Look Now. Printed and bound by BALTO Print in Lithuania.

WORLD POETRY

Marie-Noëlle Agniau
The Escapades
tr. Jesse Hover Amar

Jean-Paul Auxeméry
Selected Poems
tr. Nathaniel Tarn

Boethius
The Poems from On the Consolation of Philosophy
tr. Peter Glassgold

Maria Borio
Transparencies
tr. Danielle Pieratti

Jeannette L. Clariond
Goddesses of Water
tr. Samantha Schnee

Jacques Darras
John Scotus Eriugena at Laon
tr. Richard Sieburth

Mario dell'Arco
Day Lasts Forever: Selected Poems
tr. Marc Alan Di Martino

Marie de Quatrebarbes
The Vitals
tr. Aiden Farrell

Olivia Elias
Chaos, Crossing
tr. Kareem James Abu-Zeid

Gastón Fernández
Apparent Breviary
tr. KM Cascia

Jerzy Ficowski
Everything I Don't Know
tr. Jennifer Grotz & Piotr Sommer
PEN AWARD FOR POETRY IN TRANSLATION

Antonio Gamoneda
Book of the Cold
tr. Katherine M. Hedeen & Víctor Rodríguez Núñez

Mireille Gansel
Soul House
tr. Joan Seliger Sidney

Óscar García Sierra
Houston, I'm the problem
tr. Carmen Yus Quintero

Phoebe Giannisi
Homerica
tr. Brian Sneeden

Zuzanna Ginczanka
On Centaurs & Other Poems
tr. Alex Braslavsky

Julien Gracq
Abounding Freedom
tr. Alice Yang

Leeladhar Jagoori
What of the Earth Was Saved
tr. Matt Reeck

Nakedness Is My End: Poems from the Greek Anthology
tr. Edmund Keeley

Jazra Khaleed
The Light That Burns Us
ed. Karen Van Dyck

Judith Kiros
O
tr. Kira Josefsson

Dimitra Kotoula
The Slow Horizon That Breathes
tr. Maria Nazos

Maria Laina
Hers
tr. Karen Van Dyck

Maria Laina
Rose Fear
tr. Sarah McCann

Perrin Langda
A Few Microseconds on Earth
tr. Pauline Levy Valensi

Afrizal Malna
Document Shredding Museum
tr. Daniel Owen

Joyce Mansour
In the Glittering Maw: Selected Poems
tr. C. Francis Fisher

Manuel Maples Arce
Stridentist Poems
tr. KM Cascia

Ennio Moltedo
Night
tr. Marguerite Feitlowitz

Meret Oppenheim
The Loveliest Vowel Empties: Collected Poems
tr. Kathleen Heil

Giovanni Pascoli
Last Dream
tr. Geoffrey Brock
RAIZISS/DE PALCHI TRANSLATION AWARD

Gabriel Pomerand
Saint Ghetto of the Loans
tr. Michael Kasper & Bhamati Viswanathan

Liliana Ponce
Theory of the Voice and Dream
tr. Michael Martin Shea

Rainer Maria Rilke
Where the Paths Do Not Go
tr. Burton Pike

Amelia Rosselli
Document
tr. Roberta Antognini & Deborah Woodard

Elisabeth Rynell
Night Talks
tr. Rika Lesser

Waly Salomão
Border Fare
tr. Maryam Monalisa Gharavi

George Sarantaris
Abyss and Song: Selected Poems
tr. Pria Louka

George Seferis
Book of Exercises II
tr. Jennifer R. Kellogg

Seo Jung Hak
The Cheapest France in Town
tr. Megan Sungyoon

Ardengo Soffici
Simultaneities & Lyric Chemisms
tr. Olivia E. Sears

Paul Verlaine
Before Wisdom: The Early Poems
tr. Keith Waldrop & K.A. Hays

Witold Wirpsza
Apotheosis of Music
tr. Frank L. Vigoda

Uljana Wolf
kochanie, today i bought bread
tr. Greg Nissan

Ye Lijun
My Mountain Country
tr. Fiona Sze-Lorrain

Verónica Zondek
Cold Fire
tr. Katherine Silver